Caring for your Companion Pet - A Guide for Growers

by Karen Wren

The ultimate comprehensive guide for caring for your companion pet rabbit
from choosing the right rabbit to feeding the correct diet, providing the best accommodation and treating common health conditions.

Written by a pet owner and enthusiast breeder with nearly 50 years experience of furry companion pets.

Copyright © Karen Wren 2021.
All Rights Reserved.
No part of this book, or any portion thereof, may be reproduced or used in any manner whatsoever without the express written permission of the author.

All photography by the author except where stated.

About the Author

Karen has been a dedicated slave to small furries from childhood, starting with her first guinea-pig before gradually switching to rabbits and now focuses exclusively on large breed French Lops.

Her days consist of a routine revolving solely around 'the furry mob' who have taken over her life while providing constant amusement, ongoing bunny-education, excitement at births and watching litters progress but also occasional heartache when a much-loved furry friend is lost.
Karen is well-known for her rabbits and is locally referred to as 'The Rabbit Lady'!

She is also involved in some fundraising activities for rescue and re-homing rabbits.

Dedication

This book is dedicated to my husband for his continuous ongoing support for my projects as well as helping to lug heavy feed sacks and assisting with poo transportation for processing into organic veg - to feed back to the rabbits.

To all the rabbits I have ever been owned by - thank you for teaching me all I know about rabbits and, even after all these years, still continuing to educate me.

Contents

About Rabbits...9
Choosing your new rabbit 11
   Popular Breeds 14
      Giant breeds: British Giant or Continental Giant........................14
      French Lop 15
      Dwarf Lop 15
      Mini Lop..16
      Dutch 16
      English Angora..17
      Cashmere Lop 17
      Lionhead..18
      Netherland Dwarf..18
      Cross-breed...19
   Coat Colours..20
      Black...20
      Steel..21
      Siamese Sable...21
      Orange 22
      Sooty-fawn 22
      Sooty fawn butterfly...23
      Chinchilla...23
      Ruby-eyed white/Albino 24
      Blue eyed white..24
      Blue 24
      Opal..25
      Agouti...26
      Frosty Point..27
   Coat Patterns 28
      Self 28
      Butterfly pattern 28
      Mantle Pattern 29
      Harlequin..29
      Otter Pattern 30
      Fox pattern..31
Adopting a companion pet rabbit..32
   Male or Female?..32
   How to sex rabbits...36

Hypospadias 37
Hermaphroditism 37
Where to buy your bunny from 38
  Pet shops 38
  Re-homing Centres 39
  Responsible breeder 39
  Buying your bunny - checklist 39
  What to look for 40
  Your rabbit's parents 42
  Comparison of rabbits reared by 43
  and adopted from different sources 43
Rabbit Care Equipment 50
  Water bottle vs. water bowl 51
Housing your rabbit 55
  Outdoor hutches and pens 55
  Making your own outdoor rabbit hutch 58
  A simple, practical pen design: 62
  Indoor Cages 65
Settling in 68
Handling your new rabbit 69
  How to pick up a rabbit 72
    Fluff removal from clothing! 77
House and litter-training your rabbit 78
  House-rabbits 78
  Litter Training 80
  Rabbit-proofing your home 84
Feeding your rabbit 86
    Vitamin and mineral requirements: 86
    Mix vs. pellets? 87
      Importance of dietary fibre 88
    Which plants are safe to feed to rabbits? 93
      Safe plants: 94
      Toxic plants: 94
Rabbit Toys 96
Caring for your rabbit 99
  Coat care 99
  Moulting 99
  Grooming 101
  How to groom your rabbit 102
  Coat Clipping 103

  Claw clipping 104
  Bathing your rabbit 105
Rabbit Behaviour 108
  Diurnal Rhythms 108
  Play 108
  Chinning 109
  Chewing 109
  Exercise 110
  Digging 110
  Submission 112
  Aggression 113
  Cuddles 114
  Nose Rubs 115
  Begging for treats 115
  'Playing dead' 116
  Going for a walk 117
    Leads and Harnesses 117
Neutering your rabbit 121
  Identifying gender: 121
  Pregnancy Prevention 122
  Prevention of spraying 123
  Prevention of uterine cancer 123
  Behavioural reasons 125
  Turfing 126
Bonding Rabbits 127
  A Group of Rabbits: 128
  Introducing a New Rabbit 131
  Our bonding methods 133
  Pairing rabbits with guinea pigs? 134
Introduction to rabbit-breeding 135
  Suitable parents? 136
  Compatible colours? 136
  Mating and Fertility cycle 137
  Palpating a pregnancy 138
  Nesting 138
  Delivery 139
  Hand-rearing baby rabbits 142
Showing or Exhibiting Rabbits 145
  Judging 147
Rabbit Health 149

Behavioural changes - 150
Signs of possible illness- 150
Rabbit Health insurance 152
Abscesses 153
    Abscess treatment 154
    Home treatment 154
    Progress of an erupting abscess 155
Digestive disorders 157
    Overview 157
Coccidiosis 158
Diarrhoea 160
    Mild diarrhoea 160
    Severe diarrhoea 161
    Diarrhoea and dietary change 162
Gastric Stasis 163
    Caecotrophy 163
    Vet visit checklist - examination 165
    Vet visit checklist - treatment 166
    * In an emergency... 168
'Fur-balls' 170
    Malt pastes 172
Simple remedies available for digestive problems 172
    Probiotics 172
    Oral rehydration 172
    Protexin Fibreplex 173
    Protexin Pro-Kolin+ 173
    Science Recovery Plus 173
Syringe-feeding 174
Sticky Bottom 176
Eye disorders 178
    Cataracts 178
    Chronic Conjunctivitis 179
    Eye Ulcers 181
Neurological Disorders 183
    Epilepsy 185
    Floppy Bunny Syndrome 186
    Head Tilt (Torticollis) 187
    Paralysis 189
Fly strike (Myasis) 191
Heat Stroke 194

- Infections 197
  - Pasteurella Multocida 197
  - Pneumonia 198
- Skin and fur problems 199
  - Moulting 199
  - Simple cuts 200
  - Sore hocks (feet) 201
  - Mites 204
  - Cheyletiella Parasitovorax 205
  - Fur Mites 205
  - Ear Mites 206
  - Mite Treatment 206
  - Fleas 206
  - Home treatments for fleas and mites 207
- Teeth and dental issues 208
  - Teeth and jaw anatomy 208
  - Spurs 210
  - Malocclusion 211
  - Tooth fracture 212
- Urinary problems 214
  - Bladder sludge 214
  - Urine Scald 215
- Vaccinations 217
  - Myxomatosis 217
  - Rabbit Viral Haemorrhagic Disease (VHD-1, VHD-2) 220
- When it's time to say Goodbye 221
  - Euthanasia 221
  - Cremation 222

About Rabbits...

Welcome to the wonderful world of companion pet rabbits!

Gone are the days when a rabbit was seen as a low-maintenance pet who could be locked into a small hutch at the foot of the garden and forgotten about in-between sporadic feeding and cleaning. In contrast, today's much-loved rabbits lead pampered lives in large, spacious, airy hutches or indoors as house-rabbits often having the complete run of their owner's home.

Rabbit popularity has soared so rabbits are now the third most popular pet in the UK and rising, particularly amongst young adult professionals who long for a furry companion but don't always have the time and space to accommodate a dog or cat into their homes or lifestyles. Instead, a rabbit is an ideal alternative, being clean, quiet, tidy, fun to watch and play with and are easily litter-trained. The larger breeds, especially French Lops, are highly-interactive, responsive pets who bond closely with their owners. Most breeds, including even the largest, can live happily a small flat and it has even been suggested that rabbits may overtake the dog as the UK's most popular companion pet.

Vastly improved diets have lead to longer lifespans and overall healthier pets. Veterinary training has improved too with an increasing number of vets now taking an interest in and caring for rabbits as companion pets.

The aim of this book is to provide all the information you need to care for your new rabbit and offer him/her the best possible life with you. This includes choosing the right rabbit, handling him correctly, providing optimum accommodation, a nutritious diet, the best quality of life and, if the time comes, nursing your rabbit through illness and knowing when to seek veterinary help.

Unlike nearly every other bunny book on the market, this guide is aimed at adults and older teenagers so it includes far more detail than the rest to help you make the most of your companion pet rabbit and enjoy your lives together.

Choosing your new rabbit

As the third most popular pet in the UK, rabbits easily fit into today's busy lifestyles of working long and often irregular hours, whether commuting or working from home. They can live happily in smaller houses, flats or studios with or without a garden making rabbits equally suitable pets whether living in a town, city or countryside.

Rabbits are affectionate, responsive and interactive and can fit into your routine with more flexibility than a dog and whereas a dog requires regular walks throughout the day, a rabbit will happily use a litter tray and exercise around your home. Hence their popularity has escalated over recent years and they are expected to overtake dogs in the UK pet popularity stakes with an increasing number already enjoying luxurious lives as pampered house-rabbits.

One of the first decisions to make is the size of rabbit to adopt as these can vary from the 1kg Netherland Dwarf to the Giant breeds which can weigh more than 8kg. Smaller rabbits tend to be more skittish while the large breeds can be more placid but these are usually far too large to be handled by a child and this can risk injury to the rabbit.

Small rabbits are easy to care for...

Small rabbits are easy to care for, need smaller cages/hutches and less exercise and generally have a longer life-expectancy while the large breeds are usually better as free-range house-rabbits and cost a lot more to feed. However, there is a general rule that the bigger the rabbit – the more friendly, affectionate and docile s/he is, providing they have been well-bred and correctly reared of course!

Different breeds of rabbit can have quite different personalities and characteristics. A good, reputable breeder will know his/her rabbits and their personality characteristics and will be able to guide you and help you choose the most suitable rabbit for your requirements.

A well-bred, well-handled and socialised rabbit of any breed should make a suitable pet but we strongly recommend you choose your new furry friend carefully as you are making a lifetime commitment to your furry friend/s.

Large breeds can be ideal house-rabbits

Popular Breeds

This page shows just a few of the most popular breeds. Probably the most popular of all are Mini Lops and Dwarf while the big, lovable French Lops are often perfect rabbits for adults and ideally-suited to life indoors as house-rabbits.

This is not an exhaustive list but a brief overview of some of the most popular breeds in the UK breeds

Giant breeds: British Giant or Continental Giant

Large breed rabbits with a more slender body and head shape than the chunkier French Lops. Giants have a strong and powerful frame and weigh a minimum of 5kg up to over 10kg. They tend to be active rabbits with a long slender body of at least 65cm length, long legs and upright ears.

They are ideal pets for adults but not suited to becoming pets for children due to their heavy weight and large size. They need large accommodation and are ideally suited to being free-range house-rabbits.

Continental Giants are larger, stronger and have a more powerful frame than the smaller British Giants.

Left: Continental Giant; Right: British Giant

French Lop

A large, heavy, docile, placid and extremely affectionate breed weighing a minimum of 4.5kg but averaging 6-7kg. They have a very thickset build with chunky head and lopped ears.

French Lops make superb house-rabbits and many enjoy walks on a lead and harness. They are ideal pets for adults but less-suited to becoming pets for children due to their heavy weight and large size. They have a deserved reputation for being amongst the most docile and affectionate of all breeds.

Dwarf Lop

A medium-sized breed with a chunky build, broad head and cobby body shape. As adults, they weigh about 2-2.4kg. They are one of the most popular breeds and very popular pets for children and adults alike. With their lopped ears they have an undeniable 'cute' appeal.

Mini Lop

A very popular and appealing small breed being almost a smaller version of the Dwarf Lop. As adults they weigh about 1.5-1.6kg.

They are a very popular breed making excellent pets for children or adults and very easy to keep. Mini Lops tend to make much better pets than Netherland Dwarf for owners insistent upon a small breed.

Dutch

A small/medium sized breed weighing about 2-2.5kg characterised by their white shoulders and nose stripe.

English Angora

A medium-sized breed weighing about 2.5-3.5kg. They have a broad head, upright ears with tufty ear furnishings at the tips. Most striking is their long, dense, woolly coat which requires extensive daily grooming to ensure it doesn't become matted. In view of their grooming requirement, they are more suited to adults or older children.

Angora rabbits make excellent house-rabbits and their woolly coat is ideal for life indoors as it not only tends to receive greater attention but is less prone to becoming tangled in the cleaner environment of the home. The coat can be clipped back to about 1" for easier maintenance.

Hattie – an English Angora devoid of ear tufts

Cashmere Lop

The Cashmere Lop is a long-furred variation on the Dwarf Lop with an average weight of about 1.8-2.4kg.

Most notable is the long, silky coat which has 'fluff appeal' especially to young children but requires daily grooming to keep it in top condition and prevent clumpy mats forming. In view of their grooming requirement, they are more suited to adults or older children.

Lionhead

A relatively new and popular breed with a short, cobby body, broad head and weight of about 1.3-1.7kg. The main characteristic features are the mane of fur around the neck and skirt around the hind quarters.

The lionhead needs occasional help in grooming their mane and skirt but not the extensive grooming required by Cashmere Lops and Angora so could be a good compromise for those looking for a 'fluffy' longer-furred breed but with a more manageable coat.

Netherland Dwarf

A small breed weighing just 1kg when fully grown.

Being a small breed, they are very easy to care for and can be very hardy rabbits with a long life-expectancy extending into teenage years. However, they can also be a little 'skittish' in their behaviour so don't always make the best pets.

Due to their small size and more skittish behaviour, they are less suited to life as free-range house-rabbits but could live happily indoors with an indoor case and pen.

Siamese sable Netherland Dwarf

Cross-breed

These can be any size, colour, shape and ears can be lopped, upright or somewhere in-between! Crossbreeds are usually found in pet shops or bred by 'back-garden breeders' and may be the result of an accidental mating.

If lucky, cross-breeds can be hardy rabbits combining the best of two breeds but there is also a high risk that matings might have been inappropriate using a poor combination of parents so cross-breeding, or adopting cross-bred rabbits, should be undertaken with care.

There is likely to be little background on them so are best avoided if you have very specific preferences in terms of size or shape. Unless you see both parents, you cannot be certain exactly who you are adopting or what s/he will grow into!

Coat Colours

This page illustrates a selection of some popular colours and patterns of domestic pet rabbits.

Descriptions are based upon the Breed Standards set by the British Rabbit Council and photographs are for illustration only.

Black

A rich, lustrous, deep colour carried down to the skin with a blue under-colour. Should be free from white hairs or flecking. Black coats are usually soft and silky to touch, very glossy in appearance with a high sheen.

Steel

Left: self steel; Right: steel butterfly

Dark steel grey merging to a blue undercolour evenly ticked with black guard hairs. Each individual fur strand is banded along its length which gives the overall mottled appearance, just like agouti, opal and chinchilla.

Siamese Sable

Rich sepia coloured ears, face, back, outside of legs and upper side of tail - fading to a lighter undercolour. Paler than saddle on lower flanks, chest and belly. Eyes have a distinct ruby glow.

Orange

A sandy-orange coat with white undercolour down to the skin. White tummy, under the chin and under the tail.

Sooty-fawn

Also known as Madagascar or Tortoiseshell. Rich orange-brown colour gradually shading to blue/black on the flanks. Blue tummy and under-tail. Ears and muzzle are blueish-black.

Sooty fawn butterfly

As sooty fawn – but in an attractive tri-colour butterfly pattern.

Chinchilla

The overall colour effect is a banded blend of black and pearl giving a mottled grey appearance. Each fur strand should be dark blue at the base followed by a narrower band of pearl, with black line edging. The top should be grey and brightly ticked with black hairs and the nape of the neck should be lighter than the rest of the body.

Ruby-eyed white/Albino

Solid white fur all over and pink eyes. Albino coats are usually very soft and silky.

Blue eyed white

A white coat and striking clear blue eyes

Blue

Deep, solid slate blue colour carried down to the skin. Blue coats can sometimes have a poorer 'feel' than some other colours - e.g. glossy black and silky albino. Some blue coats may feel thick and woolly which is technically a fault in breeding/showing terms.

Opal

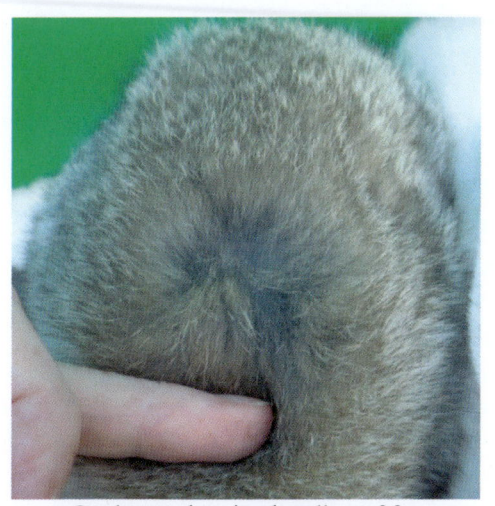

Opal coat showing banding of fur

The top colour is a mottled pale blue with a fawn band between the top colour and slate blue undercolour. The nape of the neck is light ginger. Eye circles, tummy and undertail are white.

Above: opal butterfly

Agouti

The colour of wild rabbits.

Below: **A wild rabbit** for comparison

A rich orange/yellow chestnut shade with black ticking and a dark slate blue undercolour. Like steel and chinchilla colours, each individual fur strand is banded with several colours along the length giving an overall mottled appearance.

Frosty Point

The coat is predominantly white but with grey frosting to the ears, nose, tail and variable light frosting to the back. When approaching moult, the coat takes on a 'marbled' appearance.

Coat Patterns

Coats can be a single colour known as 'self' or a mix of several colours with distinct markings, e.g. the butterfly pattern, or banded fur as found in chinchilla, agouti and steel coats where each fur strand is several colours giving an overall mottled appearance.

Self

a single coat colour (orange)

Butterfly pattern

Left: Blue butterfly; Right: agouti butterfly and sooty-fawn butterfly

White with a standardised 'butterfly' pattern of any permitted colour. There should be a distinct butterfly-shaped 'smut' pattern on the nose (or shading as per sooty-fawn), coloured ears and a small spot to each side of the shoulders. The smut should be whole without any white spots, i.e. a putty nose or moustache-like markings known as a 'charlie'. *(Think of Charlie Chaplin's moustache...)*

Mantle Pattern

Left: Blue mantle, Right: Orange mantle

A coloured body with white underbody, paws and hind feet

Harlequin

Harlequin coat pattern should be evenly divided with on side black and the other golden orange - and this pattern carries through from the head, face, ears, across the body and underneath on the tummy.

(Please note: the rabbits photographed are imperfectly marked and intended only to give an impression of the pattern.)

Otter Pattern

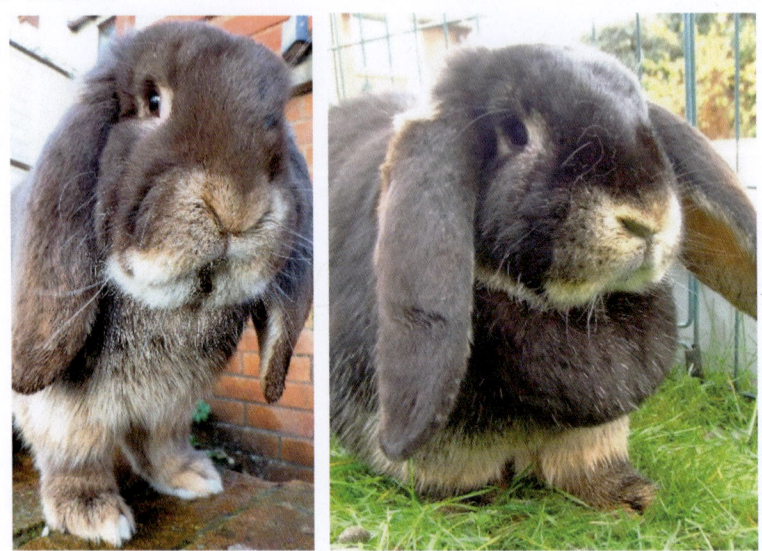

Left: Chocolate otter;   Right: Black otter

Coloured back and sides but creamy white underbody, chin and undertail. A tan border divides the white and the colour, encircle the eyes, nostrils and under the chin.   Otter pattern can also be combined with butterfly, e.g. to produce a very attractive black otter butterfly:

Black otter butterfly

Fox pattern

If the tan border of the otter pattern (above) is white then this is known as the 'Fox' pattern.

Black fox

Adopting a companion pet rabbit

Having chosen your size and breed of rabbit it is time to decide whether you would like a boy, girl, pair or group and consider whether he/she/they will live indoors or out. Then is it time to start your journey to adopting your new furry friend(s).

Male or Female?

Male and female rabbits each have advantages and disadvantages, although much depends upon the temperament of the individual rabbit, the character and temperament of both parents and, most importantly, his/her early 'rabbithood' experiences can all have an influence.

Males (bucks) tend to make better and more amenable pets. They usually form a closer bond with their owner, especially female owners, and can be much more affectionate. Although they tend to be tidier and easier to litter-train, the downside is that they can hover around a female owner's ankles making honking noises, spray urine with a very accurate aim and are more likely to become amorous with brushes, fluffy slippers, soft toys and human limbs! While walking around the garden, our boys love to weave their way around my ankles determined to trip me up – and have sometimes succeeded.

Two adult males housed together are likely to fight, although docile litter-mates who have been together from birth can *sometimes* remain good friends. However, anyone adopting two males together, who must be litter-mates, must be prepared to have them both neutered in the future and have the space to house them separately if this proves necessary, which is likely.

Females (does) generally tend to be less-tidy in their cages/hutches than male-rabbits and can go through a hormonally-induced process of 'turfing' whereby they dig the contents of their food bowls, litter tray, hay rack etc. into a large heap and urinate on it – their method of spreading their scent in order to attract the attentions of a handsome young stud-rabbit!

Female rabbits often enjoy digging burrows in your garden which can be either shallow scrapings, just deep enough to twist your ankle in, or they may tunnel beneath your neighbour' boundary fence and emerge in the middle of their neatly manicured showpiece lawn.

Spaying your girl-rabbit once she has reached puberty can prevent such hormonal behaviour, along with any territorial tendencies. However, spaying is not always *essential* although it is strongly recommended and encouraged by vets. On balance, we feel it is advisable.

Note: If you are housing two uncastrated males together, it is advisable **not** to have any unspayed does within 'smelling distance' as this can encourage spraying and sexual frustration.

Pubescent or un-mated females can become irritable (rabbit-'PMT'?!), have false pregnancies whereby they build a nest and pluck out their fur and may dig a burrow in your garden.

Unlike other female animals, rabbits do not visibly come into 'season' and females tend to be more aggressive and territorial than males. Two or more females can happily live together and they interact well in small groups. However, there is a risk of unspayed hormonal females fighting and they are likely to have more false pregnancies, but these can be prevented by spaying.

Once bred, the character of a female rabbit can change as their hormones seem to become much more activated and they develop overtly sexual behaviour which can include a randy girl spraying her owner with an accurate aim many male-rabbits would be envious of.

Bred-females often tend to become very messy in their hutches and may dig in their food bowls mixing it with the contents of their dug-out litter trays, then spraying it all and it takes only a matter of minutes for a freshly-cleaned hutch to become a smelly mess again. The girls seem to proudly relish it while their despairing owner sets to work with the shovels once again before the procedure is repeated by their brazen hussy-rabbit. This is known as 'turfing' and is thought to be their method of attracting the amorous attentions of randy boy-rabbits…..

Above: Maddie has carefully shunted all her bedding to one side of her indoor cage!

However, these are only generalisations and their background, breeding and personality characteristics are much more important factors when choosing your new pet(s).

When rabbits are adopted, you should ask their breeder/re-homing centre or pet shop staff (don't rely on their accuracy though - not all know how to sex rabbits) to show you how to identify the difference between males and females. If you are adopting a pair of opposite sexes then we stress the importance of having one neutered, usually the male because this is a very simple operation.

Once the testicles descend at puberty, then this is the time to book an **immediate** appointment with the vet and, remember, a mature male who is neutered weeks or months following puberty, can remain fertile for up to a 4-5 weeks following his castration so will need to be kept apart from any unspayed females. If a male is neutered immediately he reaches puberty, i.e. within about 2 weeks of filled testicles dropping, then there is no need to separate him from his female bonded partner for 4-5 weeks.

Note: Puberty can be as early as 10 weeks in a male - so please keep a very close eye on his nether regions, particularly if he has access to an unspayed doe!!

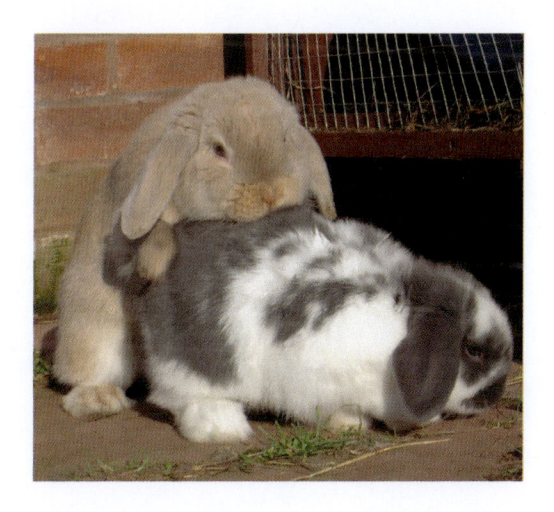

If your vet refuses to castrate a 3-4 month old rabbit then please don't take chances but *simply find a more rabbit-savvy vet* who will probably operate immediately. Generally, it is the less rabbit-savvy who are reluctant to perform this simple operation and it can also reflect those with less experience and confidence.

How to sex rabbits

We sex our baby rabbits within a day or two following birth when the gender differences can be clearly seen, although good eyesight is needed. However, this is much easier once the rabbit reaches 3 weeks of age when the genitals are much clearer and more developed.

The signs to look for when sexing a rabbit are shown on the following photographs.

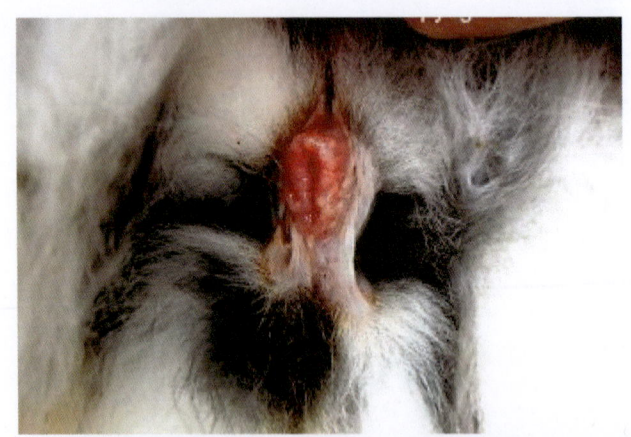

Female: A very obvious slit-shaped opening with scent glands either side

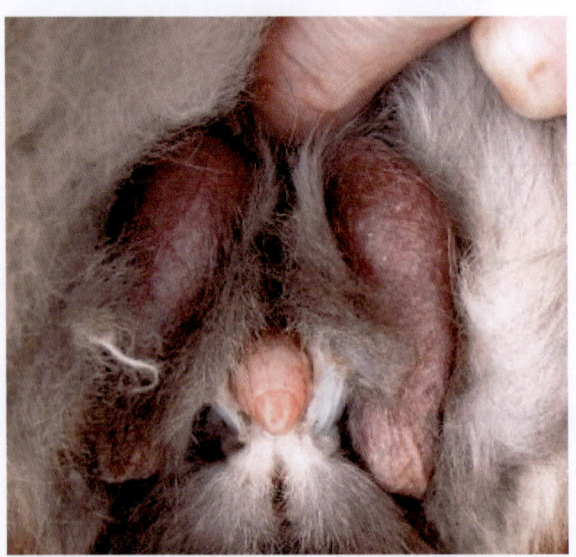

Male: Very clear testicles and penis with scent glands to each side.

Hypospadias

Occasionally a male can exhibit a 'split penis', a birth defect whereby the tip appears to have a 'slit' closely resembling the slit of the female's vulval opening and this can make accurate sexing of a young rabbit much more of a challenge. In these cases it is more difficult to be absolutely certain of the gender of a young baby. However, cases are very few and far between.

As the genitals develop, the gender will become much more obvious, especially when the testicles appear making sexing conclusive. In the case of a 'split penis' male, following puberty a 'slit' down the underside of the penis will be very apparent when he has an erection. The condition can sometimes affect fertility and because it's a defect, bucks with hypospadias should not be bred from.

Hermaphroditism

Extremely rarely it is possible for a rabbit to be born with both male and female reproductive organs.

Out of the thousands and rabbits we have owned or known over nearly 50 years, we have known two cases which have been confirmed by vets undertaking neutering surgery. Both appeared to be girls at birth, possibly had unconfirmed hypospadias but then developed tiny testicles which were removed at the same time as undergoing routine spay surgery.

Where to buy your bunny from

We strongly recommend that you choose your new rabbit from either a reputable breeder or a rescue/re-homing centre – never a pet shop.

In order to select the best rabbit to meet your needs and preferences, please consider the following:

Are you looking for an indoor or outdoor rabbit? Would you like a large or small breed, male or female or a bonded pair? Are you looking for youngsters or able to offer love and support to needy rabbits from a rescue/re-homing centre? There are many factors to consider and this book will aim to guide you through the process to choose the best rabbit(s) to match your lifestyle and preferences.

Pet shops

Just as you would not buy a puppy or a kitten from a pet shop, please do not automatically think of a pet shop as being the best source because very often this is not the case at all. Many pet shops have little, if any, knowledge of the rabbit's background and provide little advice relating to his/her care. There tends to be no after-sales service and you may find you have adopted a rabbit you cannot be fully certain of.

Re-homing Centres

Rescue and re-homing centres are another source and often have a mix of adults and youngsters needing good homes. Some rabbits may have behavioural or health problems but the centre staff, many of whom are often dedicated volunteers, will be able to advise on these so you can make an informed decision regarding which of their rabbits will be best-suited to your needs, preferences and home environment.

Responsible breeder

Generally, rabbits which have been gently and correctly handled by their breeder regularly from a young age make very much better pets than those who haven't been handled and they have little fear or apprehension towards humans.

A reputable and knowledgeable enthusiast breeder *(not a commercial breeder supplying the pet trade)* who knows their own rabbits well will be a much better source. This way you are more likely to choose healthy a healthy pet and receive adequate advice in choosing the best rabbit to suit your needs. You should be able to view the parents and possibly other relatives too, learn about the litter's upbringing and receive full advice including feeding information.

In contrast, rabbits which have been bred in confined spaces or dingy sheds with little exposure to daylight, little handling or little/no exercise outside their hutch will be much more timid, nervous and jumpy. Such rabbits can be frightened of humans and bite. These rabbits are not recommended as pets, and especially not as *companion* pets.

Buying your bunny - checklist

When adopting your companion pet rabbit, there are some facts you should be aware of:

- His/her age/date of birth - useful for insurance/vet records
- How s/he has been reared
- Diet fed to date – to avoid risk of possible tummy upset
- Whether s/he is socialised
- Character and personality
- Parentage - always ask to see the parents

- Health/fitness of parents
- Breed
- Adult size - to indicate the likely size when fully grown

- because you will be making a commitment to this rabbit for, perhaps, the next 8-10 years....

Adopting a rabbit is a responsibility - just like a cat or dog and must always be a considered decision and not an impulse purchase. A rabbit can live for 10 years and being housed in isolation or 'forgotten' at the foot of the garden, confined to a small hutch, is no way for any social animal to live.

What to look for

When adopting your new rabbit, look for:-

* The overall environment the rabbits are housed in - including daylight, ventilation, exercise outside the hutch etc.
- Clean hutches and bedding
- Clean food bowls and water bottles - food bowls should be filled with fresh unsoiled food and water bottles should be filled daily with clean, fresh water rather than just 'topped up' which can encourage algae growth
- Check the type of food the rabbits eat - i.e. a good quality pellets in preference to a muesli-style mix
- Check whether litter-trays are used and regularly cleaned. A litter-trained rabbit is greatly preferable for a house-rabbit.
- Do droppings look large, well-formed and fibrous?
- * Check the condition of the rabbit carefully, noting the following:
- Check the upper and lower front teeth are correctly aligned when viewed from the front, the teeth should be straight and the upper incisors should over lap the lower incisors. They must not touch because this is a sign of malocclusion and can lead to eating difficulties as well as regular ongoing dental bills.

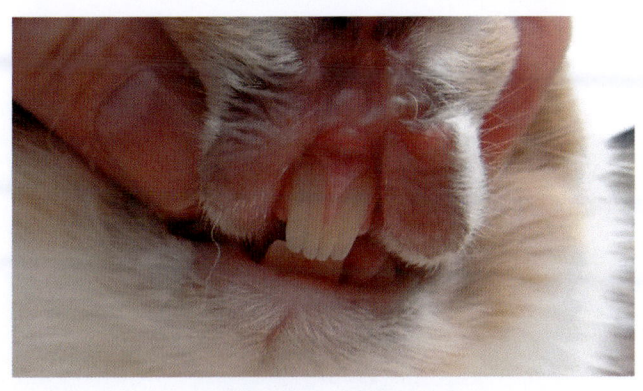

Correct incisor alignment

- The abdomen should feel plump, 'doughy', but not bloated, droppings should be firm and well-formed, the eyes must be bright, the ears and nose clean and dry, a clean bottom and the rabbit should appear alert, inquisitive and keen to explore the surroundings.
- The rabbit should also be well-hydrated which can be checked simply by plucking the scruff which should spring back instantly. If not, then s/he is probably masking signs of illness (or neglect).

* As their breeder/regular handler approaches, watch to see if the rabbits run towards him/her, stay put, or scurry away in fear (as many timid rabbits in pet shops do) and sit nervously huddled in a corner trembling. Handle the rabbit, if you can, to see how s/he settles in your arms but please note that all rabbits may be a little jumpy in the arms of an unfamiliar stranger. Their behaviour with their breeder/handler is much more representative of their normal character and personality - and how they will later bond with you. Not many rabbits enjoy being sexed and can wriggle uncomfortably but they should soon settle down once their 'bits' have been examined.

Please note: Many responsible breeders will be reluctant to allow you to handle a rabbit if it is to be returned to the litter and its mother. This is a genuine safeguard in the interests of the rabbit(s), adopter and breeder since it is possible to transmit some infections by contact and baby rabbits have very immature immune systems. Some adopters might handle rabbits at their own homes or in pet shops and then visit a breeder thus potentially carrying infections between locations. Therefore, please do not take offence if the breeder does not allow you to handle the rabbit.

However, on the day you actually collect your rabbit(s), you should then fully examine him/her to check health and general condition before accepting him/her/them. You can also be confident that the rabbit has not previously been handled by lots of strangers but only by the breeder/handler who will be kind and gentle towards him/her and is therefore unlikely to have negative experiences of being roughly handled or mis-handled.

Always choose a well-mannered rabbit...

Your rabbit's parents

 * If possible, ask to see both parents - particularly the mother. This can give a good indication of the size the baby rabbit is likely to grow to while the mother can give an idea of how its personality may develop. Offspring of nervous parents can be nervous themselves while a mother who enjoys handling is likely to produce babies which are good for handling. Also, by seeing the mother, you can judge how intensively the rabbits are bred i.e. is she pregnant again before her current litter is weaned?

Comparison of rabbits reared by and adopted from different sources

	Commercially-bred rabbits sold to pet shops	**Back garden breeder**	**Responsible hobbyist/ enthusiast breeder**	**Rescue/ Re-homing Centre**
How they're bred	Bred and sold solely for profit as a business activity. Sold to the pet trade i.e. pet shops. Might also be sold to labs for animal testing or for meat.	Often bred by accident or for 'fun' by children in a family household. Probably no profits made.	No profits made. Revenue from sales contributes towards feed bill and healthcare.	No profits made. Revenue from sales contributes towards feed bill and healthcare.
Possibility of faults of health problems	Possibly carrying defects. Are less likely to be thoroughly examined or their long-term future known.	Quite likely. Parents may be incompatible. Breeding more likely to be undertaken by owners with little or no experience and little knowledge of breed standards, faults and/or genetic defects. Parents and offspring may be carrying known or unknown genetic faults which an average pet owner might have missed - or problems may show up later (e.g. maloccluded jaws).	Considerably less risk of defects as breeders tend to focus on breeding from their best lines. Usually bred from quality parents as part of planned breeding programme. Faults are unlikely.	Faults are more likely due to background of rabbits, i.e. poor socialisation, incompatible pairings.

	Commercially-bred rabbits sold to pet shops	**Back garden breeder**	**Responsible hobbyist/ enthusiast breeder**	**Rescue/ Re-homing Centre**
Breeder involvement and rearing of litters	Breeder will probably have little, if any, involvement in the litter Babies can be taken from parents to warehouse/depot for distribution to pet stores. Within the pet store, many breeds may be mixed together to offer choice to shop customer.	Often they will have been regularly handled, particularly if there are children in the household and they have been involved in watching he litter grow and progress - and handled them gently.	Owner will probably spend much time observing and interacting with the litter and regularly handling and examining the babies.	N/A - unless kits are born at re-homing centre where they are likely to receive much attention from staff.
Background and ancestry of the rabbits	Purchasers are unlikely to be given any background on the rabbits, their parentage, source, rearing and possibly not even their diet.	Immediate ancestry will be known - although it's probable that the litter might not be the best quality. Both parents should be available for viewing.	Full ancestry and background should be available with adopter able to view both parents, previous generations and other relatives so prospective adopters will be able to judge size and health of breed.	Mostly unknown background and ancestry. Parents unlikely to be available unless babies were born on the premises or the family were taken in together by the rescue/re-homing centre.

	Commercially-bred rabbits sold to pet shops	**Back garden breeder**	**Responsible hobbyist/ enthusiast breeder**	**Rescue/ Re-homing Centre**
Environment pre-sale	Rabbits live in stores, often in a tiny cage/pen until bought. Rabbits from different breeders might be mixed together - thus increasing risks of cross-infections. From depot, rabbits are transported to stores. Health problems may not be identified.	Babies remain with mother until moving to a new home. Often just one litter to choose from. If you visit the owner's home having seen a 'small ad' then you might feel pressurised or obliged to adopt. Health problems may not be identified.	Babies remain with mother until weaned then mother is usually removed from the litter to allow them to be observed eating and drinking without suckling from her. Only when the breeder is happy that the youngsters are a good size, weight and are feeding well will the baby be allowed to move into his/her new home. Rabbits should be very healthy.	Rabbits may have health problems but the rescue/re-homing centre should be aware of these and able to advice prospective adopters of any medical requirement or special care needed.
Sexing	Sexing is not always accurate. Some pet shop staff haven't a clue how to sex a young rabbit! Staff will seldom advise on different breeds or try to ensure you're buying the size/breed of rabbit you prefer	Sexing is often inaccurate. Sometimes it is the poor sexing ability which has led to the arrival of an accidental litter.	Sexing should be accurate. A good breeder will also show you how to sex rabbits correctly - which can be done from birth.	Sexing should be accurate by experienced staff or dedicated volunteers.

	Commercially-bred rabbits sold to pet shops	**Back garden breeder**	**Responsible hobbyist/ enthusiast breeder**	**Rescue/ Re-homing Centre**
Advice available	Little advice can be given by shop staff re rabbit's characters - as they will know little of this or the rabbit's background.

Often staff cannot advise on the rabbit's diet prior to being received by the store

Little background on the rabbit made available to purchaser | Can advise on which feeds litter have been reared but these might not be the optimum diet for the rabbits. Advice available is likely to be limited and some might not be reliable or well-informed. | A good breeder will take the time to help you choose a breed of rabbit who will match your preferences and lifestyle.

Some breeders specialise in just one breed but others will have a few breeds.

Most dedicated hobbyists will have no more than 3 main breeds - excluding their 'old favourites', i.e. their retirees and non-breeding buns.

Can advise on likely character of rabbit as the line and both parents, plus previous litters and generations will be known.

Extensive care, feeding, handling, healthcare, housing and ongoing advice should be available. Breeder should be able to give comprehensive advice on breeds and which breeds will be suitable for adopter.

Can advise on which feeds litter have been reared, give good dietary advice. | Advice on care, feeding, housing etc. should be available. Adopters will probably need to have a pre-adoption home-check to confirm home environment is suitable and the rabbit/s to be adopted will be suitable. |

	Commercially-bred rabbits sold to pet shops	**Back garden breeder**	**Responsible hobbyist/ enthusiast breeder**	**Rescue/ Re-homing Centre**
Post adoption experience	Rabbit moves into new home and receives first handling, cuddles, fuss and attention - but there's a high probability the rabbit is unsocialised and doesn't enjoy this or know how to respond. Inexperienced pet owners may find the rabbit is not the snuggly pet they hoped for. The novelty could wear off as rabbit is too timid to be handled and eventually is taken to a re-homing centre if lucky or neglected if not. Every stage of the above scenario is potentially very stressful to the young rabbit who could experience 3-4 changes of environment and diet within less than 2 weeks. This stress can manifest itself in illness or dietary upset, often informally referred to as 'pet shop disease' - and this can be fatal. If not, the rabbit is unlikely to be the happiest, most-relaxed rabbit.	Rabbits are likely to settle in quickly if they have been well-handled.	Rabbits are likely to settle in quickly if they have been well-handled.	Rabbits are likely to settle in quickly if they have been well-handled. However, some can be nervous or timid having had a poor start in life, neglect or abuse from former owners. A large proportion, or even the majority of unwanted rabbits in many rescue centres are originally 'pet shop' purchases where children have lost interest or found the rabbits, often commercially bred for the pet trade, didn't meet expectations and was found to be unsocialised, nervous and didn't like being handled.

	Commercially-bred rabbits sold to pet shops	Back garden breeder	Responsible hobbyist/ enthusiast breeder	Rescue/ Re-homing Centre
Vaccinations	Not usually vaccinated at time of sale	Not usually vaccinated at time of sale	Vaccination can usually be arranged if the rabbits are not already vaccinated following weaning.	Rabbits are usually vaccination prior to adoption.
Neutering	Rabbits are normally sold as babies so will not be neutered.	Rabbits are normally sold as babies so will not be neutered.	Rabbits are normally sold as babies so will not be neutered.	Rabbits are normally sold already neutered.
Guarantee and after-sales support	48 hour guarantee sometimes available

Usually no after-sales service | Usually no after-sales advice. Many 'back garden' breeders simply do not have the necessary knowledge or experience to be able to offer information or comprehensive care advice | Most breeders usually offer 48 hour guarantee

After-sales advice often available throughout the rabbit's entire life with contact telephone number incase of any problems or emergencies | Centres will usually offer some post-adoption support and advice. |

	Commercially-bred rabbits sold to pet shops	**Back garden breeder**	**Responsible hobbyist/ enthusiast breeder**	**Rescue/ Re-homing Centre**
Recommended?	Many pet rabbit owners are cautious of buying rabbits, or any other pet, from pet shops due to their unknown parentage, ancestry, background and poor advice.	Can be good pets if they've been well-handled but there might be longer-term health issues.	Recommended. The best chance of obtaining a quality, well-bred rabbit with full knowledge of its background, parents, rearing and diet and ongoing advice and support. Some breeders are more responsible and ethical than others, so choose a responsible and caring, reputable breeder carefully.	Recommended, especially from a moral standpoint and for experienced pet owners prepared to work with rabbits who might be nervous, timid or have health problems.

There will always be variations between breeders, pet shops and rescue/re-homing centres some of which are very good while others may be very poor. The above is for guidance only.

Rabbit Care Equipment

Before adopting your rabbit, you will need to obtain certain items to adequately house your new pet/s to enable them to live a happy, comfortable life with ample space to exercise, enjoy a well-balanced diet and live a pampered life with you.

- **A suitable outdoor hutch/house or indoor cage:** appropriate size **at least** 6-8' long if your small-medium sized rabbit is to spend long periods confined to a hutch each day. Larger breeds such as French Lops will need more space, ideally 8-10' long as a minimum x 2' wide while even larger and more active breeds, such as Continental Giants, will benefit from about 10-12' long x 2' wide. These larger breeds also need much greater height to enable them to stand and groom themselves adequately. Alternatively, you may prefer your rabbit to live indoors either free-range with their own allocated space/room or to have an indoor cage to which a playpen can be attached to provide additional space for a non free-range rabbit.
- **Outdoor exercise pen** - unless you can provide a secure indoor/outdoor exercise area. Again, please buy or make a large run to provide adequate exercise so that your rabbit can run and jump. This should be at least 8' x 6' for a small/medium-sized rabbit. Most of the commercial runs from pet shops are inadequate, but you can buy two and join them together to create a larger pen. If you don't have access to a patio garden or lawn, you can still take your rabbit out for a walk using a lead and harness, or simply ensure they have plenty exercise space with you indoors.
- **Litter-tray** if you would like your rabbit to be/remain litter-trained. Few shop-purchased rabbits are litter-trained especially those who may have been 'factory produced' or mass-reared commercially in large sheds or barns. The hooded 'igloo' type litter trays intended for cats are ideal for larger rabbits and offer space to turn around and dig. We use IKEA Samla storage boxes 78x56x18cm which make excellent litter trays and beds.
- **Food bowl** - preferably a heavy earthenware bowl which cannot be easily tipped over or worn as headwear. Traditional 'Dog' bowls are ideal and a 6" bowl is a good size for a small-medium breed or an 8" bowl for large-breed rabbits. If you have a

socially aware 'woke' rabbit who is offended by the DOG lettering then you can obliterate it with a marker pen and replace it with his name instead.

Water bottle vs. water bowl

We recommend bottles in preference to bowls because:
1. It is easier to monitor water intake,
2. Bowls can be tipped over and
3. Water bowls can be easily soiled by dirty paws and ears
4. Health reasons including damp dewlaps

The exception is for rabbits suffering with dental issues or a sore mouth whereby licking the bottle spout causes further soreness and they would benefit from a water bowl instead.

Soiling via the ears is common with lop-eared rabbits who tend to dangle their ears in their bowls, sweep them along the floor then re-dangle them in their bowls and contaminating their drinking water while other rabbits will sit in their litter tray then pop their paws into their drinking water. This also applies to the large dewlaps, particularly of older female rabbits, who have a large hanging dewlap which can dangle into the bowl. Not only is this unhygienic but the wetness on the skin makes it prone to bacterial or fungal infection hence bottles are strongly advised.

Valved bottles tend to be better than the spouted type with a ball bearing because these tend to drip unless a vacuum is created inside the bottle.

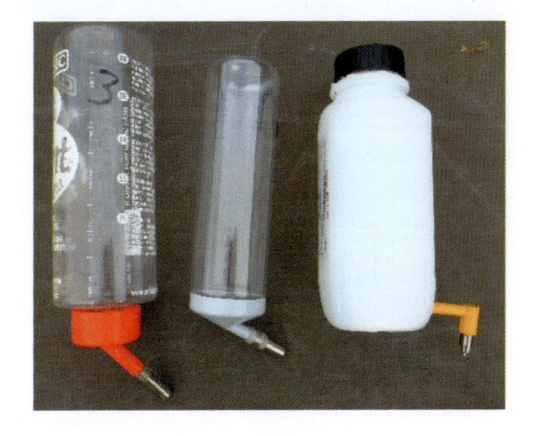

Please ensure the water supply does not freeze in winter frosts or become warm in hot weather. If it does – it needs replacing immediately. We recommend you purchase two bottles and always have these in use. Should the spout/valve become blocked or fail to operate then your rabbit can use the second bottle and won't be without water until you notice the fault. Also, in heavy winter frosts, you can bring one indoors to thaw out in a bowl while the other is in use. Then swap them over.

- **Litter** - soft, fine absorbent **wood-shavings, Aubiose (shredded hemp) or other litter** to use within the litter-tray. Some rabbit owners use non-clumping cat litter such as wood pellets which disintegrate into sawdust when wet. Supreme Tumblefresh bedding is excellent for indoor rabbits and very effectively absorbs urine odours. Please do not use clumping cat litter. If this is ingested then it can cause a nasty, and potentially fatal. intestinal blockage.
- **Bedding material** - chopped **straw** or soft barley straw is best with extra **hay** used as a dietary supplement. Please do not use wheat straw because this can have sharp ends which can cause eye injuries.
- **Rabbit pellets** – always choose a brand with a suitable level of protein for your rabbit's breed, size and age. Pellets are preferable to the muesli mixes and prevent selective feeding to ensure your rabbit has a nutritionally-balanced diet. Your rabbit's breeder will be able to advise the pellets your rabbit has been reared on.
- **Hay** - is the most important part of your rabbit's diet so always choose good quality hay. The best type to buy is usually a fresh bale from a farm used to supplying horses. Avoid any hay which feels damp, dusty, smells musty or has signs of blue mould. Much pre-packed, branded hay in plastic bags sold via pet shops tends to be poor quality and stale so always check carefully when buying to ensure is looks green, dry and smells fresh. Good sources of hay online include the Dust-Free Hay Company, Hay Experts, Hay Box or Kimberley Meadow Hay.
- **Comb/brush/slicker** for grooming (essential for longer-haired breeds); **scissors** or **pet clippers** are also recommended for Angora rabbits and human hair clippers work very well – just

wipe off any fluff before husband spots they've been unofficially shared... Shedding combs are very effective in removing loose fluff and especially during moults.

- **Salt licks** – although these are not an essential part of the diet, they can help satisfy a rabbit's craving for salt and although seldom used today (2021), rabbits seem to enjoy licking at these salt wheels
- **Hay rack: wire vs. wood.** Hay racks keep hay (for eating) off the hutch floor and prevent it becoming soiled. There are two main types including a wire cradle design which hooks onto cage bars or wire and often incorporates a loop for hanging a salt lick. Alternatively, wooden hay racks with dowelling bars to the front tend to be larger and free-standing or can be shaped e.g. into a hay wagon. Bear in mind that the dowelling is likely to be chewed.

- Small breeds love to sit in their hay rack, treating it like a cradle but ensure they cannot trap their legs in it when jumping out. If there is any risk of this happening, please either remove it, use the lidded type which cannot be sat in or replace the wire hay rack with a wooden one instead. Whilst snuggled into it, rabbits munch on the hay, enjoy a snooze and some will only hop out once it's empty.
- **Shovel, scraper, dustpan/brush** etc. for cleaning and sacks for waste, or you could use it as quality compost. Even if you don't use it yourself, some local gardeners or allotment holders might be very grateful for it. Rabbit manure advertised on Freecycle or allotments will often attract a stream of eager enquirers wanting it to fertilise their veg crops. Better still, most will collect it too making used litter disposal very easy for you.
- **Disinfectant** suitable for hutch and accessory cleaning. Virkon S is a good one for rabbits.
- **Contact details for your nearest rabbit-savvy Veterinary** Surgeon - essential because you never know when you might need them in an emergency. Please ensure your chosen vet has experience with rabbits. It is worth asking how many rabbits they see per week/month, how many neutering operations they perform along with my usual question: 'do I need to withhold my rabbit's breakfast before surgery?' If they instruct you to starve your rabbit before surgery – RUN! This is poor advice and would be a warning sign that the vet is not a bunny expert.

Housing your rabbit

Outdoor hutches and pens

Rabbits may be housed either outdoors in a sheltered area of the garden or live indoors as house-rabbits.

When considering your hutch and run design, please **Think Big!**

French Lops relaxing in their 10' hutch

Rabbits may be housed either outdoors in a sheltered area of the garden or live indoors as house-rabbits.

Please buy or make the largest hutch you can and remember that although a baby rabbit will be relatively small at eight weeks old, by the time s/he is an adult, s/he is likely to have multiplied in size many times (depending on the breed) so please bear this in mind, both when choosing your rabbit/s and their accommodation and 'Think Big' re the latter!

Rabbits are designed for exercise so the more space your rabbits have, then the happier they will be and any hutch must be at least 4 times the length of an adult rabbit when fully stretched out. All rabbits must have several hours of exercise outside their hutch every day to prevent health problems, such as muscle wastage and osteoporosis setting in. It is also essential for their general mental health and well-being since solitary rabbits confined to a small cage are especially prone to boredom.

Small and small-medium sized (i.e. up to dwarf lop size) rabbits living outdoors will require a hutch of 6-8' long and 2' deep as a minimum in addition to a larger exercise area. Many of the typical cheap, flimsy 'pet shop' hutches of just 14" depth are inadequate as your rabbit will be forced to sit diagonally! Larger breeds require considerably more space - e.g. French Lops will need a hutch of 8-10 long x 2' high x 2' deep as a minimum and at least 10-12' would be a comfortable size for Giant breeds .

The 3' hutches still sold by some pet shops are far too cramped for all rabbit breeds. As a rough guide, when fully-grown your rabbit must be able to do at least 4 rabbit-hops along the length of his hutch and be able to stand up on his/her hind legs without touching the roof. The hutch should be at least 4 times the length of an adult rabbit when s/he is fully stretched out. Approximately 25-30% of outdoor hutches should be divided into 'sleeping quarters' (though this area is more commonly preferred as the toilet area) and must be weather-proof to provide protection from wind, rain and the sun.

Another option to using a conventional hutch is to use a chicken coop which you can walk into to sit with your rabbits. These have a roof to keep the ground dry, can be stood on a base of plywood, decking, tarmac or concrete and include a large, raised enclosed weatherproof area to one side with additional external access for cleaning (although intended for collecting eggs).

Other alternatives could include a child's Wendy House or a simple garden shed, both with access to a safe, sheltered outdoor run.

Rabbits cope well with cold and frost but draughts and wet weather can cause a rabbit to chill which can lead to illness so always ensure your rabbit **always** has access to a clean, dry, draught-proof area. To enable air to circulate and prevent your rabbit chilling on a cold floor in winter, the hutch should be raised at least 6" from the ground. In the summer, your rabbit must always have access to shade – remember your rabbit cannot remove her fur coat in hot weather! A rabbit can rapidly overheat once the temperature reaches or exceeds 25°C and develop potentially-fatal heat stroke.

The floor should be lined with a layer of absorbent and insulating wood shavings, Aubiose or other litter (not sawdust which can irritate eyes and ears), with a thick layer of hay or straw to provide warmth. The remaining 70-75% should be carpeted with wood-shavings. Your rabbit will probably soil only one corner of the hutch and wood-shavings in this area should be replaced daily. Alternatively, a litter tray lined with shavings could be placed in this corner, for convenience for ease of cleaning and to keep the hutch dry. Non-litter bedding should be replaced weekly or more frequently if it becomes soiled.

In very cold weather, the hutch can be covered with bubble wrap or a piece of carpet covered by a plastic sheet to provide additional protection against the elements, especially overnight when temperatures plummet. However, air circulation and ventilation is still important so please do not 'seal' the hutch but keep a small open area so your rabbit can breath, then remove at least some of the covering during the daytime so your rabbits can enjoy some daylight. Snugglesafe microwaveable heatpads which retain their warmth for up to 12 hours, can also be useful. In very cold weather, we add a few underneath straw bedding to provide a little extra gentle warmth.

Some rabbit-keepers, often Americans or UK breeders of Angora, like to use mesh-floored hutches. These can be useful for large rabbits who are not litter trained because urine and droppings pass through the mesh to the rabbit is never sitting in his/her own excrement. However, they can be cold and draughty in inclement weather such as British winters and can lead to sore hocks in rabbits with lightly-furred paws or a heavy body weight, so we do not recommend them. Rabbits housed on mesh will need a timber platform or similar: plastic dog beds filled with hay and straw are excellent for providing a cosy, comfortable corner for your rabbit to relax in.

Combined hutches and runs, whereby the hutch is placed on the run and connected by a ramp is a highly practical option which gives your rabbit/s extra freedom and shelter in inclement weather with the option to choose whether to hop indoors or out. Just be mindful of the angle of any ramp because some can be quite steep and don't allow much of a turning space at the top or foot, particularly for a large rabbit who might need to do a 3-point turn.

Making your own outdoor rabbit hutch

Building your own hutch has the advantage of being able to build it to your own specifications to suit your rabbit and it can grow with him/her. It will probably also be cheaper in the long run as some of the 'pet shop' type hutches are constructed from very thin plywood which is prone to cracking beneath their weight and rots very quickly. Some especially poor hutches are even made from OSB strandboard which soon disintegrates once they become soaked by rain or urine. They might be cheaper to buy initially but this is a false economy if they fall to bits a few months later!

When designing a hutch, always consider the practicalities of

- Cleaning – avoid ridges at the front so bedding can be easily brushed out
- Easy access for your rabbits.
- Weather-proofing – including a canopy or overhang over any meshed doors or windows to prevent draughts or rain pouring in. It can also help preserve hutch life.
- Shade – provide a shaded area. A hutch/run must be capable of being moved to a shaded area in hot weather
- Safety – ensuring there are no sharp corners or rough edges.
- Durability – ensure plywood edges are not exposed to the weather or any damp which will hasten rotting
- Chewing – always ensure any framing is external or it will be chewed
- Security – fitting wire to both sides of any framing help make it more predator (fox) proof.
- Lockable – if your rabbits are at risk of theft.

Below is a sample of a simple hutch/run design to house 2 small/medium sized rabbits such as Netherland Dwarf, dwarf lops, mini lops, Dutch or mini rex. Larger breeds such as French Lops and Giants will need more space but, ideally, these are more suited to living as free-range house rabbits or in an adapted garden shed with an attached run.

Features include:

- Sloping roof with overhang to front and sides
- Hinged doors to front allowing easy access for cleaning
- Base of mesh door to be at least 6cm deep to prevent bedding being kicked out!
- Enclosed weatherproof area - approx 1/3 of hutch width
- Run beneath hutch connected by ramp (with grooves)
- Hinged roof to run can have either mesh or plywood covering
- 6-10 cm base to opening door to prevent food etc. spilling out
- No 'lip' on the front floors - for easy cleaning onto a shovel

Front elevation (not to scale):

Side elevation (not to scale):

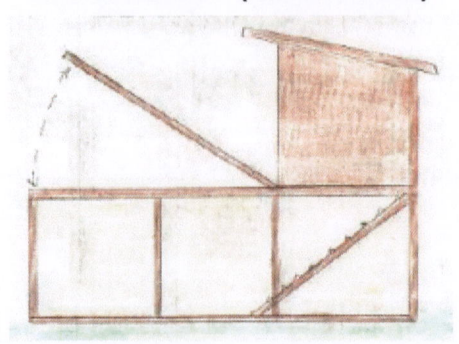

Note the roof overhang on the hutch above the run.
This is essential in wet weather.

Rabbits can thump loudly at night so use ¾" plywood for the hutch floor both to support their weight to reduce the 'drumming' and reverberations associated with thinner plywood. Hardwood is recommended. although it is more expensive.

The hutch above the run provides some shelter for wet weather but, for a hutch used all year round, then additional side panels made from clear Perspex, except in full sun or the run will become a greenhouse conducive to developing heat stroke, or plywood should be added to provide shelter from wind and rain.

All timber framing should be external to ensure it cannot be chewed. External framing also makes for easier cleaning and could be painted black to make a feature of it for 'cottage' style homes.

Adding a mesh base is a desirable addition for safety and is essential for female rabbits. Use mesh of 1" gauge or even larger loops which can be stapled to the frame. This will allow your rabbits to trim your lawn without digging an escape route out!

The run roof could be hinged to open as illustrated in a smaller run but could be heavy and cumbersome for a 6' run or larger. In these cases, we recommend fixing a felted flat or slightly sloping plywood roof for the second third and making a hinged roof to cover the final third. Alternatively, a lift-off roof for the pen which can be secured via cabin hooks or bolts once in place.

Notes:

Please use hinges, not pins, for the opening doors. The pins as used on some cramped, budget pet shop hutches create a 1" gap between door frames in which paws or youngster's necks can become trapped.

Ensure any plywood is treated with a preservative which is safe for animals such as Cuprinol Timbercare for internal wood and Cuprinol Ducksback (other preservatives are available) for external wood.

Below, is a manufactured hutch 6' long x 2' wide x 4' tall which is occupied by two mini lop occupants. Below the hutch is a ramp to a lower exercise area in addition to an attached run (out of shot).

The 8' below hutch is occupied by the two litter-mates. Normally it is on legs to raise it from the ground, thus allowing air to circulate and prevent the floor becoming too chilly in cold weather. This hutch is inside a 16x10' enclosed pen.

A simple, practical pen design:

The run photographed is 6' long, 3' wide and 2' tall and constructed from hardwood with the wire mesh fitted to the inside which prevents the timbers being chewed. The roof is made from a separate frame to which lightweight corrugated plastic panels have been fitted. The run is placed on flagstones for easy cleaning and to prevent females digging their way out!

- This run is based on a slight incline to allow rain to run off the roof – which has a 6" overhang
- Based on concrete flagstones to enable easy cleaning.
- Note the wire mesh is fitted to the **inside** of the frame to minimise chewing

A run placed on concrete/flagstones can be easier to keep clean and can be blasted with a pressure washer. The paving slabs will help keep toe-nails in check but could lead to sore hocks if your rabbit is a persistent 'thumper'. A warm, raised/insulated resting area will be needed as concrete flagstones can be very chilly to lie on. We provided plastic dog-beds filled with barley straw in cool or cold weather.

Provided your garden is well enclosed and devoid of possibly toxic plants then, with supervision, your rabbit could run loose but any rabbit could eagerly devour your prized foliage when they think you're not looking!

Walter enjoying a free-range exploration of the snow

Indoor Cages

An increasing trend is to bring your rabbit indoors to live as a house-rabbit. We always encourage this as it allows your rabbit/s to become real members of your family and you will see far more of their personality, character and benefit from increased interaction with your furry friend/s.

Rabbits can be either free-range but, if you're out at work all day and not 100% confident about leaving him/her/them to roam free, then indoor cages are available or you could confine your rabbit to one room or area using a 'baby gate'.

A baby gate ensures Wally remains in the lounge

Partitioning off a section of a room can work well so your rabbit has his/her own safe space to retreat to while you have the option of confining him/her for periods such as overnight, while decorating or when it isn't practical to be free-range. We created such as area in our upstairs home office so Tobermory has his own 10 x 6' space with indoor cage base to use as a litter tray. Because he isn't neutered and there is a risk of spraying, while waiting for him to hit puberty, we lined all the walls with Correx so that in the event of some creative 'wee art' up the walls, it would be easy to wipe clean.

Then we added a baby gate which is left open for him to come and go as he pleases but closed when he needs to be confined.

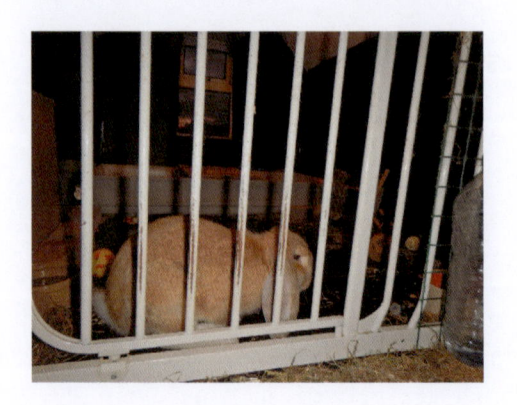

Indoor cages provide an excellent 'base' for indoor bunnies. Smaller breeds can be confined to a cage whilst unsupervised i.e. when you're out at work or overnight and fitting a play pen to the front will allow extra space for exercise and play.

A play pen fitted in front of the cage and the cage door left open will allow your rabbits the freedom to hop in and out as they wish, provide ample space for unsupervised exercise and play time - and you can rest assured knowing that your cables and best furniture are safe!

Large indoor cages can be difficult to source so another option is to join 2-3 (or more) of the standard 100cm cages alongside each other to make a 2-3m (or longer) cage. Such cages can provide a 'base' for unconfined, free-range house-rabbits to come and go as they please.

Settling in

Once you bring your new rabbit home, remember that s/he is adjusting to a new environment with new people and will need time to settle.

It's important to offer your rabbit plenty of attention as s/he get to know you but also ensure that you offer him his 'own space', such as an indoor cage, which will help with litter-training. Confining him/her to a smaller, restricted area will make litter-training and bonding much easier and also discourages any timid or skittish behaviour during the settling-in process.

This confinement to a restricted space is especially important with smaller breeds as it helps with the bonding process while also helping your new family member(s) feel more secure as s/he adapts to his/her new home, sounds, smells, surroundings then begins to explore and find his/her way around.

Tobermory explores his new bachelor pad

Handling your new rabbit

Once you have brought your new rabbit home, introduce him/her to his/her new accommodation, i.e. hutch, indoor cage, pen or shed and leave him/her to quietly settle in for a few hours following his journey home. If you have excitable young children then we advise a quiet settling-in period of 24-48 hours while still checking that he/she is eating and drinking, of course. This is less important with adult owners but is always advisable when moving to a family environment with lots of noisy young children. Many young rabbits are not used to this and it could be stressful while they adjust so it's worth allowing settling-in time.

Please encourage any young children to be calm and quiet around the new family pet since this also helps young children learn their new family member is a living animal and not an animated, cuddly toy, despite how cute s/he may appear. Also, please ensure children do not push fingers through wire mesh or cages since this can be quite intrusive for the rabbit who is settling into his own space and adjusting to his new environment. Because rabbits have poor near-vision, finger-poking may be perceived as a threat and can encourage negative behaviour or even a sharp nip from a nervous rabbit. Later, as they adjust to their new home environment, they'll enjoy the greatly increased attention and affection, and enjoy becoming the centre of attention!

Every rabbit is different and has his/her own individual personality and character along with his/her likes and dislikes which extend to food, toys and even humans. Indeed, very often you'll find your rabbit will bond most closely with one person more than another. This is especially noticeable in affectionate French Lops and Giants who can become very attached to their owner. Generally, males bond more closely with female humans and female rabbits seem to prefer a male human owner. So, when couples adopt a boy-girl pair of rabbits each will normally have a preference!!

Ensure your rabbit is eating well, drinking from his/her bottle and producing normal droppings over the next few days. Gradually start handling by introducing your hand to him/her and stroke him/her gently to allow him/her to get to know you. Once s/he seems confident with you, s/he can be picked up. To do this, support the rabbit's chest and rear end and hold him/her against your body. Gently grasping the scruff of their neck and supporting their rear end with your other hand may be easier for larger rabbits. Rabbits have relative weak spines which are prone to injury so always ensure their back is fully supported by resting it against your arm or body or hold the rabbit's body against yours.

Some rabbits are easier to handle than others. We begin our handling from a young age so ours are used to being picked up and fussed and grow up confident with being handled. Others may not be used to it, protest and prefer to be fussed at ground level so always be guided by what your rabbit is comfortable with.

In our view, we feel well-handled rabbits are easier to manage which also makes is easier to clip claws, administer medication and allow your vet to handle him without him becoming stressed.

Most pet rabbits from a good, reputable, hobbyist breeder who has spent time socialising them are generally confident from a very young age. In contrast, rabbits commercially bred for the pet trade often haven't experienced much if any human contact and tend to be timid so it can take time to build up their confidence and they will determine and set the pace for their handling.

Ensure the rabbit's spine is fully supported by taking his weight on your arm

Or hold the rabbit against your body to support his weight

Be warned: large-breed rabbits are heavy and your back is likely to feel the strain if held for long periods. It is often easier to sit when handling the larger breeds!

Each rabbit is different: some prefer to be picked up for cuddles and snuggle against their owner's chest while others prefer to sit on a knee or simply sprawl outstretched on the floor and invite you to join them. The more you give to your rabbit, the more pleasure your rabbit will give you in return and you'll quickly develop a close bond with your new furry-friend.

Commercially-bred rabbits unused to human contact can be nervous leading to fear, aggression and scratching, hence the settling-in time with slow, respectful and gradual contact is much more important. Once settled, gradually start introducing your hand to him/her and stroke him/her gently to allow him/her to get to know you. In the case of a fully-socialised rabbit, you'll probably find your progress is much faster and more rewarding as he gets to know you.

Once fully settled, don't be surprised if he wants your attention immediately, then gives you a gentle nudge if you end his fuss before he's granted permission for you to do so or go to bed *and he may even want to join you there!*

How to pick up a rabbit

Above: How to handle and pick up your rabbit securely.

Once your rabbit seems confident with you, then he/she can be picked up. Although rabbits have excellent almost 360° vision, they have a small blind spot immediately in front of them hence they often can't see their food but sniff for it instead. If you approach from directly in front, emerging from their blind spot, this can be perceived as a threat and trigger an aggressive reaction. Instead, approach from their side so your rabbit can see your hands and know you're not a threat, and then proceed to fuss and pick up your rabbit.

To do this, support the rabbit's chest (not stomach or abdomen) and rear end taking most of the body weight at the tail end. Gently grasping the scruff of their neck and supporting their rear end with your other hand may be easier for large-breed rabbits or pregnant does. Then hold the rabbit close to your body for comfort and support

Rabbits like to feel secure and can feel safest with all their four paws close against your body. This is most usual when you're wearing freshly-laundered white clothing and they've been digging deep in thick, sloppy mud!

We usually recommend you give your rabbit the fuss in the way he/she prefers. There's nothing wrong with pampering your rabbits.

Never pick up any rabbit by the ears because this can cause pain and injury

Some prefer to snuggle up to your chest while others stand on your bent forearm and 'hide' their head between your arm and ribs while the especially soppy like to rub their cheek against your own cheek for a really close and affectionate cuddle.

Most of ours like to sit on our shoulders and nibble our ears. Our larger rabbits stretch across our shoulders and drape themselves behind our necks like a head-rest but we recommend sitting down before tackling this with a generously-proportioned French Lop or Giant!

Trancing

Especially tame rabbits will lie on their backs, cradled into your elbow, with their head back and mouth dropped open almost like a hypnotic trance, allowing you to rub their chest and nose.

However.... There is a school of thought which suggests rabbits find this position stressful and blood tests have shown increased stress hormones. Long before research ever considered this, we handled our rabbits this way with no signs of any stress, anxiety or discomfort. We have continued to do so from a very young age and while they're still adopting this position naturally to nurse from their mothers. To them, it is then still a natural position and we find some of our rabbits will flop for a rest and some will even roll onto their backs to sleep with their legs in the air! They don't appear the least bit stressed. However, in light of the research findings, if your rabbit isn't used to this posture and resists it, then please don't force him/her into it. Regarding handling, your rabbit's comfort and well-being must always be the highest priority.

Your rabbit should be handled at least twice daily and will probably enjoy joining you to watch a TV film in the evenings. Some rabbits are happy to lie (with full body and head support) on their backs and allow you to gently stroke their chest and belly. Most rabbits enjoy a nose-rub either using the backs of your fingers or rubbing his nose with your own (be warned: it tickles!!) or a relaxing neck and shoulder massage behind their ears.

The more gentle handling, fuss and attention your rabbit receives, then the more you will bond with him/her. Similarly, the more time you spend with him/her then you will see more of his/her character and personality.

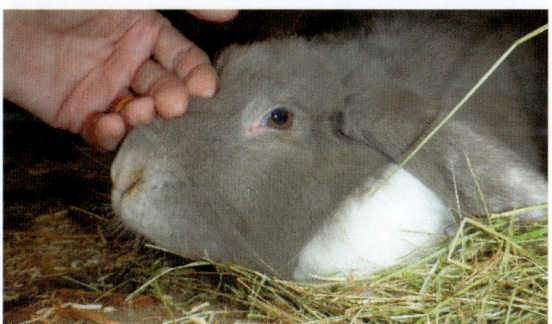

Rabbits can be surprisingly affectionate, highly interactive and all have their different personalities, habits, preferences and 'funny ways'.

On uttering the word "tiptoes", one of our house-bunnies would instantly (unless asleep) stand on his hind legs and beg for treats.

Willy begging for hand-fed treats

Others can be taught simple tricks or use stimulating toys to work out how to reach their treats which also encourages natural foraging behaviour.

Fluff removal from clothing!

Remember – rabbits can shed a lot of loose fluff when being handled so it can be a good idea to designate an old fleece jacket for snuggling your rabbit, knowing it will soon be covered in fur.

Lint rollers with sticky roller heads are very useful for quickly and effectively removing fluff from clothing. Alternatively, large pieces of packing tape or even a damp cloth will pick up loose fluff from smaller areas.

House and litter-training your rabbit

Wally, the coal-chewer
"It wasn't me...."

Gone are the days when rabbits were exclusively thought of as being pets for young children who would bide their days sitting in cramped hutches at the foot of the garden with little attention or stimulation. Instead, today's well cared-for rabbits either lead pampered lives in large hutches or, increasingly, they are being brought indoors to live warm and comfortable lives as house-rabbits. This was a phenomenon popularised in the USA in the mid-1980's and the idea has crossed the Atlantic to become an increasingly popular and fast-growing trend in the UK where today in the 2020's a house-rabbit is now considered the norm rather than a novelty.

House-rabbits

Having a house-rabbit is a very practical option on many counts: today's smaller households live in smaller homes, work longer hours, marry later and have smaller families (or no family at all), so a pet rabbit can be much more practical than a cat or dog. They provide all the benefits of having a small, furry, affectionate pet but with less mess (sometimes…) and they require less space. Living in small town/city apartments, young professional couples have neither the space required for a dog nor the time required to go for long walks so a rabbit is the perfect alternative, without being considered a 'second best'.

Rabbits can be less messy than other pets
(but I didn't say they were less tidy!)

Rabbits are clean, easily litter-trained, quiet, fun to watch and play with, surprisingly responsive and interactive, develop their own personalities and characters and are very social animals. They benefit from the company of another rabbit or a human owner and can form a very close bond with their owner – particularly male rabbits with a female owner. High profile TV celebrities also have or have had house-rabbits, including Chris and Ingrid Tarrant, Jo Brand and Toyah Wilcox whose New Zealand White rabbit, Beaton, used to snore loudly under her bed!

Rabbits can live in conventional outdoor hutches or could become house-rabbits living in a 'rabbit-proofed' home and go out for walks on their own lead and harness – just like a puppy. In fact, a 2002 survey of rabbit owners by pet insurer, PetPlan, found that 20% of their policyholders' rabbits were house-rabbits and these probably represent only the small minority.

Litter Training

Maximus (lionhead) in his litter tray

When starting litter training we advise keeping a rabbit confined to a restricted area which he will learn to recognise as his own space and an already litter trained rabbit will normally use this reliable from the outset. Then gradually increase the amount of time allowed outside this designated space as he becomes or remains litter trained.

If starting from scratch with a rabbit who has never heard of using a litter tray, then it may pay off to take a few days off work (perhaps don't tell your less-understanding colleagues the reason why!) and follow your rabbit everywhere s/he goes. Rabbits are creatures of habit and once they get used to urinating where they shouldn't, it can become a habit which is hard to break so it's easiest not to let the habit form initially.

So, as soon as s/he adopts the tell-tale squatting posture, often accompanied by staring straight into your eyes if squatting on your brand new pristine white carpet, scoop him/her up and deposit in the litter tray. Whilst there, offer nose-rubs, shoulder-massages or whatever fuss your rabbit likes best. Even when your rabbit is dozing in his/her tray and not actually using it for its intended purpose, always reward him/her. Perhaps add a bundle of hay to the clean end of the tray. What you're aiming to do is make the litter tray as comfortable and cosy as possible so that it becomes a favourite place to be enjoyed and relax in. If your rabbit enjoys spending time here, then s/he is likely to mark it as his/her territory and then use it regularly.

You might find it's easier to have a number of litter trays positioned in different corners of the room so that your rabbit can choose the one s/he prefers.

Usually when undergoing litter-training, rabbits first learn to wee in their tray which is the best news for your carpets. Later, the droppings follow into the tray but it is normal for there to be a few occasional scattered droppings outside the tray. Luckily, these are clean, odourless and non-staining and, if you happen to accidentally tread on one, it won't be squashed into your carpet but will break into a fibrous powder easily cleaned up. In the case of caecotrophs, you'll be less lucky as it's quite a challenge to scrape one of these from your shag pile or best sheepskin rug, even less so once you've trodden it around the room while your rabbit watches while failing to suppress his amused bunny grin.

During puberty, then it is normal for there to be a break-down in litter-training but once this hormonal phase is over, 'good' behaviour normally resumes again shortly.

This is also the time to consider neutering your boy-rabbit since he might start spraying now. Spraying urine, usually over his female owner, is not pleasant for the recipient and bucks can have a very accurate aim as you'll discover if you approach him with your mouth open (surprisingly, it doesn't taste quite as strong as it smells) or receive a sudden earful of warm, pungent urine. Glasses are another favourite target. If your rabbit starts to spray then we strongly recommend he is castrated as soon as possible before it becomes his favourite pastime.

Sometimes, male rabbits can be easier to litter-train than females. After puberty, females can (but don't always) become very messy in their cages/hutches if they are not spayed due to hormonally-triggered behaviour. At this time, your normally polite, neat and tidy, demure and innocent little doe can turn into a stroppy little madam who possibly becomes sporadically territorial towards her accommodation and, within this, may begin a process of 'turfing'. This involves digging the contents of her food bowl, litter tray and hay racks etc. into a large heap and she will then urinate on it and probably spray around her cage. Turfing produces a large, damp, untidy heap which harbours a strong odour of urine and is her way of telling any boy-rabbits nearby that she is ready, willing and able. If this, together with false pregnancies and frequent nest-building, becomes a problem then spaying will prevent, or at least greatly reduce, such behaviour.

If your rabbit is to become a hutch-rabbit then litter training is less critical but it is very convenient. Most prefer their litter tray to be in the enclosed 'sleeping area and it's actually quite rare to find a rabbit sleeping in his 'bedroom'. Perhaps they're shy and like to have some privacy?!

Uncovered indoor litter trays should be lined with about 2" layer of wood-shavings or other litter and stand on a further tray or sheet to catch shavings kicked out when rabbit hops out. If your rabbit doesn't immediately understand the purpose of the litter tray, scoop up a few of his/her fresh droppings and deposit these in a corner of the tray. Next time rabbit squats with his/her tail raised and that tell-tale give-away expression of concentration, scoop him/her up and gently place him/her in the tray. He/she will soon learn and regularly use the tray.

This should be emptied and cleaned daily although not too often in the early days to ensure it still smells like his/her toilet area. If it's cleaned instantly then it won't retain its soiled odour and could confuse your rabbit so it is a case of striking the right balance and then, once it's in regular use, you can clean it daily as required.

If your rabbit still doesn't understand what the litter-tray is for, then try confining him/her to a much smaller area and gradually expand as litter-training progresses. Rabbits naturally do not like to soil their living area so, when forced into a smaller area, our rabbits will deposit their droppings in one area only - and this is the spot to place the litter tray. Also ensure the rest of the hutch/cage floor is completely bare so that the tray becomes the most comfortable area of the hutch. It may look a little odd at first but it does work. Your bun won't like to paddle in urine so she'll naturally choose the most absorbent area and, hey presto, bun is litter-trained! Once the tray is in use then further bedding etc. can be added to the hutch.

Should your rabbit have 'accidents' then these should be scooped up and placed in the preferred corner of the litter tray, preferably whilst the guilty party is watching you. Similarly, should your rabbit squat down, tail raised with an expression of concentration, scoop him up, pop him in the tray and make a fuss of him while s/he continues to perform. Nose-rubs, treats, hay etc. can be used as rewards (or bribery).

If your rabbit is one who likes to back right into the rear of his/her litter tray and then aims over the top of it, either use a hooded Cat-Loo or choose one of the corner litter pans with high sides.

Once litter-trained, there might be the occasional stray dropping deposited outside the tray but often there is no need to scoop these up as your rabbit will eat them next time he/she passes them on the floor. This is perfectly normal rabbit behaviour, especially amongst house-rabbits. Caecotrophs might also be deposited in the centre of your lounge carpet but, again, your rabbit will probably return to eat these very soon and sometimes it's easier for the even the most house-proud to turn a blind eye.

Rabbit-proofing your home

Above: Vulnerable cables run through conduit

Your rabbit might chew so please ensure his/her environment is safe and there are no trailing electrical cables. These should be tucked beneath carpets, threaded through tubing (toilet overflow pipe is ideal or tough tubing can be purchased from aquatic suppliers) or taped to skirting boards to ensure they are out of temptation's way. Telephone cables are especially enjoyed so please ensure these are safely tucked out of reach. If your rabbit likes to join you to 'surf the net' or send emails to his/her rabbit-friends, please ensure the mouse cable is well out of reach - a quick nibble and you'll soon discover your mouse isn't quite as lively as your rabbit!

Above: protecting TV/monitor cables…

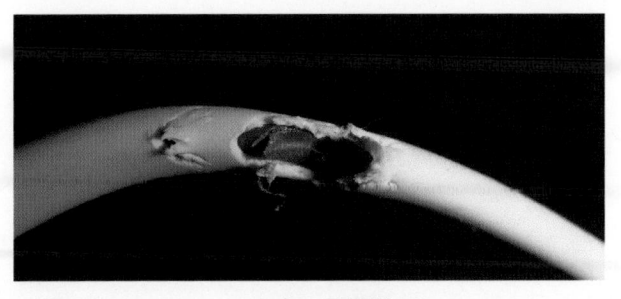

...against THIS!

If you'd like to do a more permanent job, then it's best to run cables through conduit along skirting boards and this can then be painted to blend in with your decor. Visitors might not understand why you have plumbing parts around your lounge and phone cables sealed down with duct tape, but you'll soon grow used to it and barely notice them.

As for your bed, rabbits do seem to enjoy joining their owners for a snuggle beneath the duvet. However, they also seem to like to empty their bladder, or leave a fresh pile of droppings, on the side of the duvet occupied by their closest carer, so be warned!

If your rabbit nibbles wallpaper in a favoured spot, then a clear sheet of Perspex over it will prevent this. As for carpet-chewing, we don't recommend this as part of their diet and it can indicate a craving for dietary fibre. One of our house-rabbits, Mayflower, had a special taste for our carpets which became a problem until we discovered seagrass mats which are a perfect diversion.

Chewing deterrents can include rubbing chair/table legs with soap or even a light coating of petroleum jelly. The latter works indirectly: the rabbit gets the grease on his whiskers and then wants to wash it off immediately rather than chew your table leg and by the time his whiskers are clean, he's forgotten what he wanted to gnaw. The tiniest drop of Olbas Oil or TCP can also work wonders as a one-off deterrent because many rabbits dislike the smell although your home may soon smell like a medical ward. However, do take care when using eucalyptus oil or any other essential oil because these can be toxic to pets.

Feeding your rabbit

A healthy high-fibre diet of hay and pellets

Rabbits are herbivores and should be fed a natural high fibre diet of grass, good quality hay and natural forage. Such a diet needs grinding by the molar teeth which helps to keep a rabbit's continuously growing teeth in trim while also maintaining good gut mobility.

In practice, it isn't always possible or practical to pick daily grass for your rabbit so commercially prepared rabbit feeds can supplement a largely hay and leafy diet while also providing additional protein needed by growing rabbits.

Vitamin and mineral requirements:

- Vitamin A   12,000 iu - important for fertility and the survival of young rabbits
- Vitamin B complex - this is found in grains and is reingested via soft caecotrophs

- Vitamin D   1,200 - 1,600 iu - a lack of Vitamin D can lead to calcium deficiency. Vitamin D can be synthesised by the body via UV sun rays (as in humans)
- Vitamin E   is necessary for protections against infection and an as anti-oxidant. Rabbits don't tend to be susceptible to deficiencies
- Calcium: Phosphorous ratio should be 1.5-2 calcium: 1 phosphorous. Calcium is required for the formation of strong teeth and bones as well as being involved in energy cycles. Excess calcium can lead to kidney and bladder stones.
- Magnesium should account for 0.3% of the total diet
- Very little fat is required although the fatty acid linoleic acid is essential.

Mix vs. pellets?

'Old-fashioned' muesli type mix – no longer recommended in favour of nutritionally balanced pellets

As a general guide, an ideal rabbit mix or pellet for non-breeding small-medium sized adult breeds should include: 12% protein, 1-3% oil, 0.5-1% calcium and 20% fibre. Pregnant or lactating does, growing youngsters and giant breeds can have additional requirements. A complete pellet or mix, supplemented with fresh long hay or grass, can provide a fully balanced diet. If your rabbit is producing excessive caecotrophs which she/he is not re-ingesting, then we recommend reducing the amount of concentrated feed and increasing fibre in the form of extra hay. Providing a branch to gnaw, such as apple tree or willow log, or some fresh crusty bark to strip will also help provide some additional fibre while also helping to maintain good dental health.

Importance of dietary fibre

Rabbits are herbivores and, in the wild, would consume large quantities of fibrous plant material which is essential for maintaining a rabbit's unique digestive system. Rabbits produce caecal pellets which are re-ingested to provide additional protein and 'good bacteria' beneficial to their digestive process which is ideally suited to a high fibre, low protein diet. Fibre is the most important single constituent of the rabbit diet and a lack of dietary fibre can lead to major health problems, such as gastric stasis and dental problems. Ideally, the fibre should be from abrasive grass products such as grass, alfalfa, hay or forage rather than cereals such as maize, oats, barley, wheat or corn.

Fresh, clean water must be available at all times for rabbits to drink around 50-100ml/kg per day and is best given via a water bottle for hygiene rather than a bowl since these can be tipped over or easily soiled. In the winter, ensure the water supply does not freeze. Wrapping a bottle in bubble-wrap can help prevent this but the spout may still freeze and need to be thawed out in a bucket of hot water.

A good quality, nutritionally-balanced rabbit pellet, is recommended in preference to the traditional 'muesli' type rabbit mixes fed up to about 20-30 years ago. Pellets, such as 'Burgess Excel' nuggets or 'Science Selective' pellets manufactured for small-medium sized breeds, or a higher-protein pellet produced for giant and larger breeds, should be available in a bowl. This should ideally be a heavy ceramic bowl which your rabbit will find harder to overturn, toss around or wear overturned on his head.

Although commercially prepared branded muesli-type mixes can look colourfully attractive *to rabbit owners, at least* and offer rabbits variety in their diet, these mixes also allow rabbits to be selective in the bits they eat and leave. Many rabbits prefer the flaked peas and coloured crunchy nibbles known as 'biscuits' in preference to the pellets and will leave these behind while awaiting a bowl top-up. If the essential vitamin and minerals have been added to the pellet part of the mix, then rejecting these will not provide your rabbit with a fully balanced diet. Therefore, it is advisable to only feed your rabbit once their bowl is empty (or soiled), rather than when your rabbit has selected his/her favourite elements of the mix, to ensure he/she has a balanced diet. We feed our rabbits a nutritionally balanced pellet diet but also keep a bag of muesli mix which we use for hand-feeding as a treat or for tempting ill or convalescing rabbits to eat.

Youngsters being reared on a recommended pellet diet

Feeding a pellet instead of a mix is now the advised diet for rabbits. Some pellets available from feed centres may also contain a coccidiostat to help prevent the intestinal disease, coccidiosis and these are often used by breeders with multiple rabbits although immunity to the disease can develop requiring additional medication such as Baycox for rabbits infected with coccidiosis.

Rabbits enjoy grass, clover, dandelions/leaves and clean fresh vegetables such as carrots, carrot tops, cabbage, occasional tomatoes and the odd small piece of apple, but all dietary changes must be introduced **very** gradually for young rabbits and we recommend waiting until they are 3-4 months old before doing so. Always avoid sudden changes in diet which can lead to stomach upsets and diarrhoea. In very young/small rabbits a bad attack of diarrhoea can be fatal.

A natural fibrous diet of grass and forage

    We recommend making any switch to a different brand of pellet or mix takes place over 10-14 days. To do this, add 10% of the new mix to the existing on the first 3 days. On days 4-5, add 20% of the new mix so the ratio is now 20% of the new mix to 80% of the existing. On the 6th day, this can be increased to 30%, then 40% then 50% so that after 10-14 days, the changeover is complete. When introducing grass and veg, it is advisable to do so gradually. One way of doing this would be to allow your rabbit to run on grass for 10 minutes on the first day then monitor him/her for 48 hours, then increase the time to 20 minutes on Day 3, then 30 minutes on the Day 5 and so on. Similarly, we recommend introducing veg slowly - a single slice of carrot on Day 1, then 2 slices on Day 3, half a carrot on Day 5 and so on, ensuring that you don't introduce both grass, new veg or fruit on the same days. These guidelines may sound cautious but it's better to be safe than sorry with delicate rabbit stomach. Potatoes and most types of lettuce, especially iceberg, should not be given.

    During 2001, around the time many manufacturers launched their new ranges of pellets onto the pet market making pet rabbit diets topical, there were lengthy debates questioning whether domestic pet rabbits should be fed a diet consisting solely of grass and hay. We feel that, while this could be suitable in the short-term, in the longer-term it would be imbalanced and larger breeds such as French Lops need a higher level of protein. In the wild, rabbits would also eat wild herbs, plants, weeds and tree bark thus providing a much wider food intake rather than simply grass and hay. However, this high-profile debate did emphasise the need for a high level of dietary fibre and grasses and hay which require a lot of chewing to help keep teeth in trim.

Just a note when your bunny is grazing amongst various types of grass outdoors, particularly late summer when the grasses begin to seed, always check for any signs of sharp grass seeds causing any injury to your rabbit. Seeds can become stuck in the nose leading to sneezing and nasal discharge, in the genital area causing pain, in the feet around a sore hock which can lead to infection or mouth or cheek which can lead to painful chewing and a reluctance to eat.

Rabbits require up to 16-18% crude protein throughout their lives for growth, reproduction, cell renewal and tissue repair.

Grasses and grains contain different levels of protein and fibre:

- oats, wheat, barley, maize contain 9-12% crude protein
- dried grass - 19% crude protein
- alfalfa (lucerne) - 22%
- wheatfeed (used to make crunchy biscuits found in mixes) - 17%
- Digestible protein should be 65-75% of the total crude protein

Hay provides **essential** fibre and must always be available as a staple part of the diet. This can help prevent furballs and gastric stasis disorders while the chewing action of long hay is necessary for healthy teeth. Timothy Hay, although it has limited availability in the UK, is very highly recommended for rabbits as one of the best types of hay.

We advise against much of the typical plastic-bagged, shrink-wrapped hay sold via pet shops. The plastic does not allow the hay to breathe and much of this hay is quite stale and, sometimes, dusty. It's suitable for use as bedding but not ideal as a staple part of the diet. Far better is clean, fresh, fragrant meadow hay bought from a farm, and it's usually much cheaper too. A full 20kg (approx) bale will normally retail from a farm shop for about £6-£8 and is much more economical. This tends to be good quality hay, i.e. a quality that any farmer would readily use to feed his own stock and your rabbits will undoubtedly taste the difference. If buying a fresh bale isn't practical then there are specialist hay suppliers online selling high quality hay suitable for rabbits, e.g. Dust Free Hay Company, Hay Box, Kimberley Hay, Hay Experts and the Happy Hay Company amongst others.

In addition to hay, another good source of fibre is Spillers' ReadiGrass, also known as dried grass by Friendship Estates, i.e. grass dried rapidly at a high temperature to retain the colour and seal in the nutrients. It has a high protein content (12%) together with 2% oil and a very high fibre content of 32%. This is available in 1kg bags labelled for rabbits or large 15kg bales intended for horses (or a lot of rabbits!) from animal feed stores.

Other excellent sources of fibre include: Dengie HiFi (35% fibre), Dengie HiFi Lite (35%), Dengie Alfa-A (27%) or Dodson & Horrell Fibre Blend.

A rabbit recovering from gastric stasis can benefit from a short-term diet of grass, ReadiGrass, long fresh meadow hay and water although this would not sustain a doe through pregnancy or weaning and could lead to growth retardation of very young rabbits.

Tip: One way to determine whether your rabbit has sufficient hay and fibre in his diet: crush a fresh dropping and it should crumble into a fibrous dust.

Which plants are safe to feed to rabbits?

Feeding grasses, plants or weeds can add variety to your rabbit's diet and provide essential vitamins, minerals, nutrients and dietary fibre. However these must be selected with great care because many tasty-looking plants can be quite toxic. Generally rabbits will instinctively avoid bitter or toxic plants but we feel it's a risk not worth taking so please always ensure that any plants, weeds or flowers which your rabbit might be able to reach, are safe for him/her to nibble on. They should not be treated with any weed-killers, fertilisers or pesticides or have been soiled by dogs, cats or other animals.

Rabbits will also tuck into any tasty plants in your garden so please ensure they are safe and anything potentially toxic should be kept out of reach.

Blair enjoying our sunflower plants - *once we'd turned our backs*

The following lists are for guidance only and are not exhaustive:

Safe plants:

Alfalfa, Barley, Blackberry, Clover, Coltsfoot, Comfrey, Cow Parsley, Daisies, Dandelions, Fruit trees, Hazel, Hogweed, Lucerne, Meadow Horsetail, Mint, Nettles, Plantain, Rose, Shepherd's Purse, Sow Thistle, Sunflower, Thistle, Wheat, Willow, Yarrow.

Toxic plants:

Anemone, Azalea, Bittersweet, Black Bryony, Buttercup, Box Privet, Buckthorn, Broom, Bluebells, Black Nightshade, Bindweed, Beech, Cowbane or Water Hemlock, Columbine, Celandine, Cyclamen, Cypress, Clematis, Chrysanthemums, Deadly Nightshade, Delphinium, Elder, Figwort, Foxglove, Flax, Fools Parsley, Greater Celandine, Greater Spearwort Ground Ivy, Hemlock Water Dropwort, Hellebore, Hemp, Herb Paris, Horse Radish, Holly, Hyacinth, Iris, Ivy, Laburnum, Laurel, Lupin, Lily of the Valley, Larkspur, Lesser Spearwort, Lobelia, Monkshood, Marsh Marigold, Oak, Potato, Privet , Poppy, Pimpernel, Ragwort, Rhododendron, Ramsons, St. Johns Wort, Sand wort, Soap wort, Sowbread, Sorrel, Vetch, Water Dropwort, Water Hemlock or Cowbane, White Bryony, Woody Nightshade, Wood Anemone, Wild Garlic, Yew, Yellow Flag – plus, as a rule of paw, anything grown from bulbs should be considered poisonous.

We've known rabbits happily tuck into some of the above particularly ivy, seemingly without any ill effects so, if you see your rabbit taking an illicit nibble, try not to fret. Although toxic and must be avoided, they are not necessarily going to be fatal.

We give our rabbits regular forage throughout the year including fresh dandelions and dandelion leaves plus leafy willow and chewy willow sticks to gnaw. In addition we dry dandelion leaves, raspberry leaves and blackberry leaves to feed out of season. Forage is available from good pet supplies stores or our own can be ordered from http://www.rossrabbits.co.uk.

Rabbit Toys

Toys help provide amusement and stimulation, especially for single rabbits left to entertain themselves during the day.

Toys can be very simple. Rabbits love tunnels to run through, a cardboard box with 'doors' cut into the sides, toilet roll inners and balls etc. to fling and toss around. Treat-balls stuffed with pellets, hay, straw or dried grass are excellent and help encourage natural foraging behaviour by making the rabbits 'work' for their food, gaining some exercise and stimulation in the process.

A wide range of toys, wood gnaws, salt licks, hay racks and other novelties and amusements for rabbits are available to order online and from pet supply stores. Some buns will watch in quiet amusement while you spend hours browsing online bunny toy stores, parting with your hard earned funds on a vast range of toys only for your bun to ignore them but ravage their discarded delivery box with excited enthusiasm. Well it *is* a bun's prerogative…

Outdoor rabbits, especially girls, will enjoy having an area they can dig in or a simple plastic tunnel tube to rest in.

Your rabbit may also enjoy going out for a walk and run wearing a smart lead and harness designed specifically for rabbits. Walking may be a slow process because s/he will inevitably want to stop occasionally to sniff an especially tasty plant or to have a wash. If any dogs approach then don't take risks - simply scoop up your bunny and give him a cuddle while the dog passes by.

Caring for your rabbit

Coat care

Although grooming is often overlooked it is still essential, even for shorter-furred breeds, and helps to reduce the amount of fur ingested, thus reducing the risk of furballs and blockages which can lead to blockages and gastric stasis.

Where rabbits live together in pairs or small groups, they will mutually groom each other, particularly around the face. They will also help keep minor conditions under control and we've known of several rabbits which have seemingly suddenly developed minor eye infections or runny eyes after losing their bonded companion. This is also noted to suddenly clear up once bonded with another rabbit until owners notice that the companion is keeping a persistently sticky eye clean and clear. However, areas which are hard to reach, such as just above the base of the tail, tend to be ignored so some human help will be needed to help prevent mats forming, or cutting out mats if they have already formed.

Rabbits also enjoy being preened and fussed by their owners, particularly when this is rewarded with additional cuddles and favourite treats.

Moulting

Rabbits should be groomed every few days if needed but during their bi-annual moults, they will appreciate additional help at least twice daily. Moulting usually occurs in early spring and late autumn and will start around the rabbit's nape and shoulders then spread across his back and flanks with the fluff from the belly being the last to be shed. There can be some skin irritation at this time so it's a good opportunity to check for any signs of mites or fleas.

Above: Netherland Dwarf starting to moult across his shoulders;

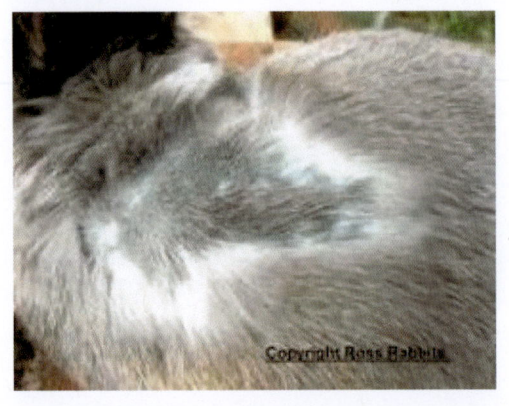

Above: the new coat growth can be clearly seen

Plucking or combing out loose fur can help prevent it being ingested leading to fur-balls. These occur when too much surplus loose fur is swallowed by your rabbit as he grooms himself. In the stomach, this combines with food and can form a huge mass which then blocks the stomach exit. As a result, the rabbit's stomach remains full and feels large although no nutrients are passing through and your rabbit is slowly starving. With the large stomach, your rabbit will feel full and stop eating and drinking and will soon begin to bloat and swell. This process can happen very quickly, particularly in warm weather when dehydration can be rapid and should be treated as a veterinary emergency.

However, the condition can be largely prevented by simple regular grooming.

Grooming

Using a shedding comb with teeth of different lengths to pull out loose fur, run this against the growth of the fur to allow air to circulate and pick up fur from the undercoat, then remove fur from the comb teeth and comb your rabbit again, this time in the direction of the fur growth. Follow each comb stroke with a stroke from your hand and you'll probably find your rabbit settles comfortably down on your knee/floor and enters a relaxing doze. Some rabbits are less keen on having their bellies groomed as this is a quite a sensitive area.

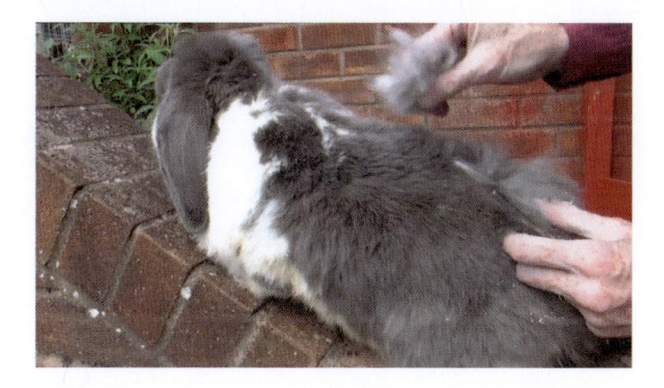

Longer-haired breeds such as Angora and Cashmere need regular grooming to help prevent their fur becoming tangled and matted. They should be trained to sit on your lap or a stable surface while you gently brush their wool or fur.

How to groom your rabbit

1. Before grooming, start by gently plucking out any loose fluff, particularly from their rear and tail area.
2. Start at the rear and back-comb against the direction of the fur growth which aids air circulation.
3. Now work up to the shoulders then start again, brushing in the direction of the fur growth, so that the coat lies flat and you'll probably notice its new, fresh, glossy appearance. The rabbit will feel the benefit and you may find it highly effective yourself for calming and general stress-relief.
4. Once you've finished, give your rabbit a big cuddle as a reward for sitting still and allowing you to groom him so thoroughly.

Your rabbit's coat should be examined twice daily to check for any conditions of concern such as excessive fur loss during a moult which could lead to fur-blockages, the possibility of mites, or soiling and staining which could attract flies leading to an attack of fly strike.

If your rabbit is prone to a sticky bottom then the fur might need to be clipped for hygiene purposes. The amount of protein in the diet should also be reduced and more grass and hay offered to provide additional fibre. In warm weather, application of a product such as 'Rear Guard' can help prevent an attack of fly strike. These conditions are summarised on the Rabbit Health pages.

Coat Clipping

Angora coats benefit from clipping in the summer

    This can be overlooked but rabbits can very easily over-heat in hot weather and no human would want to sit out in the heat of a hot summer day donning a thick wool or fur coat.

    If you have a long-furred rabbit such as a cashmere or Angora, then they will benefit from regular clipping of their coat. Unlike other rabbits which have fur coats, Angoras produce a thick coat of very fine wool which is harder for them to groom and the fine strands tend to become wrapped around the incisor teeth and can be hard to remove.

To clip your rabbit's coat, clip the fur down to about 1" all over which helps keep it manageable - although your rabbit might sulk for a while afterwards, especially if he thinks you've ruined his handsome good looks and the stunning coat he's spent months growing!

    If your prized Angoras are show-rabbits bred specifically for their coat qualities, this is a different matter and alternative methods should be found to keep your rabbits cool in hot weather. Installing air-conditioning units is the most effective method of cooling their environment or using oscillating fans should help a little for light occasional use.

Claw clipping

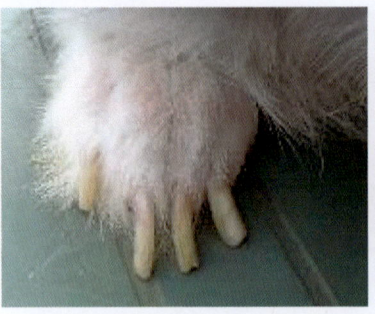

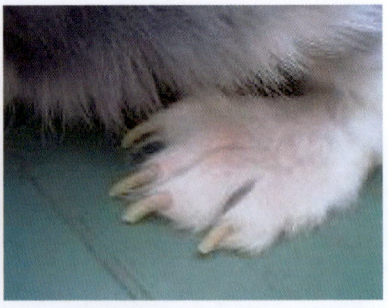

Above: overgrown toe nails

In addition to general grooming, it will also be necessary to clip your rabbit's claws occasionally. This is a very simple procedure, especially if your rabbit has white nails and the best time to check is during grooming time.

Use guillotine-action clippers designed for cats and dogs which are also suitable for rabbits. There are two ways to do this: either pop your rabbit onto a flat surface such as a wall or a table, or simply roll him onto his back to see all the claws exposed together. Look at the nail to identify the clear nail, the pink quick and the fur between the toes.

Aim to clip about 2mm past the quick, i.e. the pink area of the nail where the blood supply and nerves run. In darker nails, it's a good idea to shine a torch beneath the nail to illuminate this. Always apply gentle pressure just before you cut just to confirm you're not going to clip any nerves and have left ample space just past the quick. If your rabbit should flinch then stop immediately, then try again, cutting a little further down.

Always cut on the safe side. It is better to snip a little more off later if the claws are still too long rather than cut a nail too short and nip a blood vessel. If you do accidentally clip a nail too short then a styptic pencil will help to stop the bleeding.

If you are not sure or not completely confident about doing this, then your Vet or a vet nurse will be able to show you how to clip nails so you can do it yourself in the future.

Bathing your rabbit

Rabbits are fastidious self-groomers and normally keep their coats clean and healthy. However, occasionally your rabbit's bottom might require cleaning e.g. following an intestinal upset or severe case of urine scald. Admittedly, is not the most pleasant of jobs but should only be required very rarely, if at all.

We advise wearing a pair of rubber gloves then lower your rabbit from the waist down into a bowl of warm water containing a mild cat or rabbit shampoo. Let her body rest against your right arm while you clean her bottom with your left (gloved!) hand.

After cleaning, lift her out and smooth out excess water. Then towel her dry to remove much of the water. She will then need to be dried using a hair dryer on a low setting and may appreciate having her fur gently combed and teased into her favourite style. Always ensure her coat is dry since a damp bottom can attract flies and **Fly Strike** in warm weather or cause a chill in cold weather.

Some years ago I was asked to help bathe an elderly and arthritic bunny, Jazz, who was one of the most co-operative rabbits I've helped to clean and seemed to enjoy her bath-time, attention and following beautification.

Use a washing-up bowl filled with warm water and a mild shampoo suitable for pets

Gently dunk the bunny into the bowl cradling her on your arm. She may splash a little so waterproof clothing is advisable. Wash the affected areas - you may wish to wear a rubber glove for very messy bums!

Dry the coat as much as possible with a towel

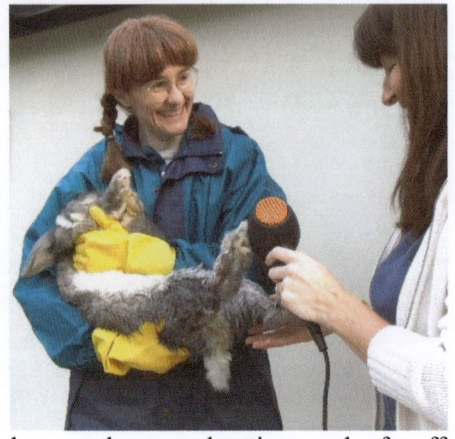

A hair dryer used on a cool setting can dry fur effectively

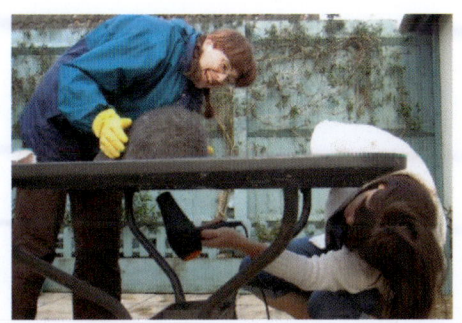

a mesh-topped table gave good access to Jazz's underside!

Once she's sporting a clean, dry sparkling bottom with a beautifully styled, sweet-smelling and freshly-groomed coat, you can be sure she'll now hop away to dig in a nice, thick, sloppy mudbank…..

Another delightful job which might you might need to do occasionally is clean out your rabbit's scent glands. These are found at each side of your rabbit's anus and secrete a very strong-smelling, dark brown waxy substance. Should the glands become blocked and swollen then they can be cleaned using a cotton bud. Be warned - the smell is revolting!

Rabbit Behaviour

A healthy, happy rabbit is naturally inquisitive and will want to explore his environment and this is often the first observation a new rabbit-owner makes. Whereas guinea-pigs will often scurry timidly away, a rabbit will take his/her time to look around, sniff at everything within reach and perhaps 'chin' a few items to add their scent, using the scent gland beneath their chin.

Rabbits are quiet and never vocal unlike guinea-pigs who will contentedly squeak all day. Instead, the only vocal sounds normally made by healthy rabbits is a loud squealing 'scream' should they be severely startled, frightened or in pain. Should there be predators or other perceived threat, then rabbits will thump firmly with their hind foot to sound the alarm as a warning for other rabbits nearby.

Diurnal Rhythms

Rabbits are crepuscular animals being more active in the early morning and late afternoon or evening. They tend to feed at these times then rest for much of the day, dozing and relaxing between around 9-5pm. This makes them especially good pets for working households who are out at work during their sleepy relaxed hours, then bright and alert when owners return home in the evening to feed and fuss them again.

Play

Rabbits love to play, particularly in small bonded groups. With the increased popularity of rabbits for adult owners, pet toy manufacturers have begun to address this unexploited market and often introduce new and expanding ranges of toys specifically designed to stimulate rabbits and help prevent boredom setting in although. Alas, often it's the owners who enjoy playing with the toys while the bored rabbits watch them in pity.

Toys can be quite simple such as pieces of wood suspended on wire, a plastic treat ball (intended for dogs) into which food treats can be inserted and will be dispensed as your bun rolls the ball around. Other items can include wood chews or something as simple as a cardboard box with holes cut into 2 sides or a tasty untreated seagrass mat which can be chewed, dragged around, scratched and generally demolished over a few weeks. Always ensure any toys offered are safe to be chewed and cannot cause any injury or be harmful if ingested.

Chinning

Rabbits, especially males, will be seen to scent-mark by chinning items around the home or garden. This is their way of marking their territory by applying their scent to it via their scent gland under the chin. Males also scent mark by spraying a well-aimed jet of urine, often onto their companion. Rabbit companions seem to tolerate this very much better than less-appreciative human companions do.

chinning plants in the garden

Chewing

Rabbits have continuously growing teeth so it is important to provide, firstly, the correct diet with lots of hay and grass to encourage your rabbit to chew and help grind down his molars to prevent painful spurs developing. Also, provide a piece of untreated wood – such as an apple tree branch or willow stick to gnaw on. It is natural for rabbits to chew to wear down their teeth, so please don't try to discourage this. But, if your rabbit starts to chew on a table leg rather than his toys or wood gnaws provided then try rubbing your furniture with soap as a deterrent and, at the same time, offer your bun a more desirable piece of edible wood, such as a small fruit tree branch, of his/her own.

Exercise

Daily exercise outside a hutch or cage is vital for general health and well-being. Rabbits need daily enrichment and enjoy having things to climb on e.g. a small plastic stool intended for toddlers can provide hours of fun, tubes and tunnels to run through e.g. large-diameter clay pipes or flower-pots from a garden centre, a tub for digging in, a ramp to run up and down and a covered area to hide in. By providing an outlet for exercise and stimulation, it is less likely that your rabbit will become bored and take his/her frustration out on your best furniture, carpet or prized book collection. You can also take your rabbit for a daily walk using a special rabbit harness together with a long lead

Providing your house/garden is rabbit-proofed then he/she can be allowed to explore, under your supervision.

Digging

Mum and daughter burrowing team

Rabbits love to dig! This is perfectly natural behaviour for females who are the natural diggers in the wild, while males might scratch around at the earth but then soon lose interest and wander off leaving this to the more proficient women-rabbits.

Hard at work….

In contrast, females are very proficient diggers and can burrow out of a run placed on grass within an hour. If you have several females, you might notice they actually form a team of diggers with one digging a deep burrow while the others concentrate on removing the earth dug out. Then they'll change over and work on a rota. It really is most impressive teamwork to watch but, if you're thinking of placing a run grass or earth then it **must** have a mesh base to prevent your rabbits tunnelling out - which they almost certainly will do.

Champion digger, Blodwyn, proudly emerges from her burrow

You might find that your rabbit also likes to dig in his/her litter-tray which can make a dreadful mess on your best carpet. To minimise this, use a covered 'Cat Loo' type litter tray with sides and a hood. Some also have a swinging door and these are even better for containing litter-tray contents.

A cardboard box with holes cut into the sides rather than the ends, also provides an excellent digging area and any mess is hurled against the end walls and remains contained until your bun has had enough and hops out again.

Submission

Mounting: a form of expressing dominance

Submission is generally shown by a rabbit lowering its head to the ground with its ears low. When introducing a new rabbit to another, one is usually more dominant than the other. In order to show who's 'Boss', human or lagomorph, simply push the aggressor's nose to the ground/floor and he/she will learn to submit to the other rabbit, or human!

Mounting, which can be either at the head or tail end, is another means of showing dominance with the dominant rabbit mounting the submissive rabbit to show that she (usually a female) is in charge.

Once rabbits are bonded, you will see them snuggled together side by side and, often, sharing mounting and grooming activities.

Aggression

Rabbits are not usually naturally aggressive animals but a lot can depend on their early rabbit-hood experiences. In our opinion, it is always best to adopt your rabbit from a family environment or breeder who handles their rabbits regularly and raises them as **pets**, rather than 'stock'. When adopting from a pet shop, generally, you'll have no idea of the rabbit's background, rearing or parents' temperaments so you are taking chances – and risks.

Often, aggression is caused by too little handling and socialisation while young or bad experiences of being handled such as being dropped and hurt. Or aggression might be related to fear such as noise, strangers or, in the case of unsprayed females, the rabbit equivalent of 'PMT'! Fear can cause aggressive behaviour which is usually in the form of a sharp nip – and it hurts!

If your rabbit is showing aggressive behaviour then the best way to treat it is to try to understand *why* and then tackle any external stress factors. If the stress is hormone-related in females, then allow them to go through this spell quietly for a few days and they should soon be back to normal again.

If your rabbit is scrabbling while on your knee and clearly doesn't want to be snuggled then it could be something as simple as a full bladder and a trip to the litter tray will relieve this and your rabbit will enjoy his/her cuddle in greater comfort afterwards. However, if s/he simply prefers to stretch out on the ground for a shoulder-massage or nose-rub, then let him/her enjoy this rather than do something they are uncomfortable with. Always reward desired behaviour with nose-rubs, rubbing your nose/chin onto his, stroking his/her ears, offering favourite treats or doing whatever your rabbit enjoys most.

If your rabbit lunges at your hand when you put it into his/her hutch then it is probably due to the rabbit feeling threatened or having its hutch/territory invaded. Rabbits have long-distance vision rather than short-sight so a hand immediately in front of their face will not be in focus and could be misconstrued as a threat. Always move your hands slowly and gently and approach your rabbit's face from the side and never from overhead. Rabbits are prey animals and would be attacked this way in the wild. Really, it all comes down to thinking from your rabbit's perspective, rather than your own, and then acting upon it.

Cuddles

Some rabbits are naturally more cuddly and snuggly than others. This is just part of their character and personality and it is up to you as their owner, aka personal slave, to learn about your rabbit and discover what he/she likes best.

A socialised rabbit who has been used to handling from birth is much more likely to enjoy being cuddled as an adult and generally, these rabbits are much more rewarding to own. Some will sit on your shoulder like a parrot, others will join you in bed, and some will sit on your knee for hours on end while others prefer you to sprawl across the floor with them. Finding what they like most is fun and most rewarding when you find your bunny becomes putty in your hands when you find his/her weak spot!

Cuddling a relaxed rabbit on your knee is very soothing and an excellent means of relieving stress. Your rabbit will probably enjoy it too but, if you become so relaxed by it and start to nod off, don't be surprised if your fingers receive a gentle nip to remind you to continue the strokes. This is not the same as a bite but more of a reminder that the fuss is reducing as you fall into your state of slumber....

Nose Rubs

Enjoying nose-rubs

Rabbits love nose rubs! Some like to be rubbed along the length of their nose up along their forehead. Others enjoy having the very tip of their nose 'button' rubbed. Yours will make it clear what s/he enjoys most!

Begging for treats

Rabbits can be surprisingly interactive and responsive to humans, will demand nose-rubs, give you a nudge when they want fuss, beg for treats and enjoy being hand-fed.

'Playing dead'

A scary habit of rabbits is giving their owners a near-heart attack by 'playing dead'. Especially relaxed rabbits perform a 'bunny flop' whereby, in a fully relaxed state, they thrown themselves onto their sides and appear to be dead. It's happened to me several times when, even after nearly 50 years of being a bunny slave, I'll see one flopped on his side looking as though he's expired and have to check by giving a gentle touch – at which point a very grumpy bunny looks up annoyed at having been woken from his slumber. One of our early dwarf lops, Posy, took this a step further with a habit of sleeping on her back.

Posy – who often slept on her back

Going for a walk

Rabbits enjoy exercise and this is essential for their general health and well-being. Just as in humans, exercise offers a good cardiac workout, helps benefit the respiratory system, builds up and tones muscle and strengthens bones. When it's not possible to run free, then your rabbit will probably enjoy being taken for a walk using a lead and harness for safety.

Leads and Harnesses

Rabbits can enjoy being taken for a walk using a lead and harness if you live in a suitably quiet area for this. Quiet country lanes are ideal or, if you live in a small town then you may have access to a quiet park. We also know some rabbits lucky enough to live on the coast who relish a skip along a quiet dog-free beach. Unfortunately, we haven't had the opportunity to offer this experience to our land-locked rabbits.

Some rabbits have nervous, timid and skittish natures and these will probably not benefit from or enjoy such an outing so are probably better left to enjoy their familiar home environment instead. Similarly, if they are the type of rabbit to become easily startled or panic by unfamiliar noises or people, then going out for a walk is probably not something they would enjoy. As a responsible owner, your judgement is needed to gauge whether your rabbit is one to enjoy exploring the great outdoors.
Others love it, especially the more docile larger breeds. Our French Lops and Giants love to hop along, explore and expect us to dutifully and obediently follow along our quiet country lanes. If they see people while out on their walks they happily sit down and enjoy being fussed by them.

Please choose a harness i.e. a harness with both a chest *and* collar strap - not just a collar which is large enough for your rabbit and, unless you'd like him/her to be forced to walk to heel with you, e.g. on a pavement, please opt for a longer lead of at least 1 metre length so that he has ample space to roam without being confined to your ankles. If your bunny is a dedicated 'chewer' then, for safety, it is advisable to replace any lightweight fabric leads for a chain version so it can't be quickly bitten through!

Obviously, a rabbit should not be walked beside a busy road with heavy traffic or lots of people about but if you live in a quiet area with almost traffic-free and people-free lanes, then this can be suitable for rabbit-walking. If a car should approach then please be prepared to shelter him from any traffic if he seems stressed by this and, should any dogs approach, then pick him up at this point for a cuddle. It's not worth taking risks, even with a dog of the friendliest appearance. A friendly-looking dog to a human, can be perceived very differently by a prey animal such as a rabbit.

If you are taking your rabbit across fields that might have been frequented by wild rabbits, then please ensure he is up to date with his myxomatosis and VHD1 and VHD2 vaccinations since these illnesses are highly infectious and transmitted very easily. However, no vaccination can ever guarantee 100% protection so it would be safer to walk your rabbit away from hedgerows or any areas where there is a known VHD or myxomatosis outbreak.

To fit your rabbit's harness, lift him onto a stable, non-slippery surface and fit the collar and chest straps. Ensure the harness fits securely around the chest and neck allowing adequate room for breathing and postural changes. We fit the chest strap first just as a precaution incase your rabbit decides to hop away - not advisable with a collar around the neck.

To check for fit, insert two fingers beneath the neck and chest bands and if you have to squeeze your fingers in then it's too tight and constrictive. Then attach the lead. Now pop your rabbit down on the ground, let him sniff around and get used the harness, without the lead attached, if it's his first time wearing it. If he's uncomfortable with it, remove it and try another day for a short period then build up gradually over a week or two until he is comfortable before heading out for your ramble together.

At first, your rabbit might be a little hesitant, try to scratch off the harness if he's never worn one before but he should be quickly grow accustomed to it. Then he'll probably sniff around and set off on a slow and faltering walk.

Hurry up, mum!

It is common for rabbits not used to going for rambles to suddenly stop dead in their tracks, to settle down and have a wash or to simply stretch out on the footpath expecting nose rubs or a shoulder massage. We tend to pamper our rabbits and, if they tell us they'd like some fuss en route then they receive it, but then we'd like them to walk a little further in return and will reward them for this too.

Once a rabbit is used to being taken for walks then you'll probably discover a rabbit can be just like an excited, enthusiastic puppy who looks forward to his walks. These will be very different to the timid and apprehensive first steps of a first walk – instead, your rabbit will tear off, ears swinging if he's a lop and you'll be dragged along behind him. Sometimes, if he's in a hospitable mood, your rabbit will be good enough to stop, look around then sit and wait for you to catch up before dashing off again.

Others seem to find it more fun to always run towards their owner which means the poor human has no choice other than to walk backwards. This is fine on a deserted lane but is not recommended on busy footpaths. If you choose a rural area for your walk then be prepared to stop for dandelion leaf treats while some neighbours' bushes can provide delicious refreshment breaks.

Afterwards, rabbit will want to check you've stayed with him and come to you for a big cuddle and, if you should ever stop en route, you'll either find yourself being dragged along or have your bun climbing up your leg, reminding you that he's still with you and wanting to carry on.

So, taking a rabbit for a walk isn't quite the same as taking a dog out for a ramble. It is much less predictable but can also be much more fun for this very reason. Also, it's a great way to make new friends since few onlookers can resist passing a comment about your rabbit on a lead.

Enjoy it – and your rabbit will, too!

Walter - who loved his daily hops around the countryside

Neutering your rabbit

A baby rabbit can be accurately sexed just a few minutes following birth so any rabbit sold after weaning should be extremely easy to sex. The only difficulties which are likely to occur are in males with hypospadias ('split penis') whereby they appear to have a female 'slit'. However, once they reach puberty, they are very clearly not female once the testicles appear.

Identifying gender:

The gender differences are clearly illustrated on the following photographs:-

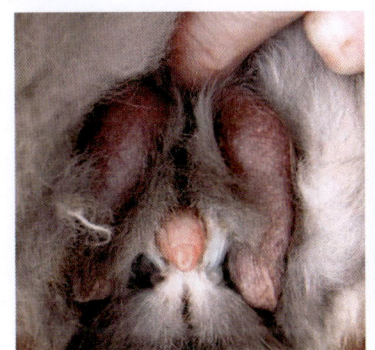

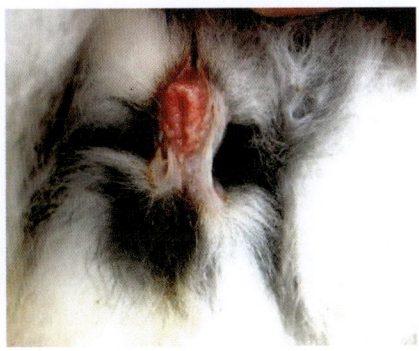

Left: male; right: female

Neutering (castration or boys or spaying of girls) is a decision to be taken by responsible and caring rabbit owners and can be based upon different factors:

- prevention of unwanted/unplanned pregnancy
- prevention of in-breeding when brother and sister live together
- the need to prevent males spraying
- prevention of uterine cancer in does
- behavioural reasons

Pregnancy Prevention

A buck and doe can reach sexual maturity at just 3 months of age so it is essential that you monitor the development of your male rabbit(s) to ensure there is no risk to your female rabbit.

If you own a male and a female rabbit who live together or might come into contact with each other by accident, then it is **essential** that one or both of them are neutered. The male castration is a very simple operation and we would personally recommend that *he* is castrated first i.e. from 12 weeks old rather than his female companion. Spaying the female is a more complex operation which can follow later, from 5 months of age, i.e. when the internal organs are larger making surgery easier. Neutering can also help in bonding rabbits who live together in groups.

There is no 'Morning After pill' for rabbits but females can be spayed following an accidental encounter and to ensure an accidental conception does not result in an unwanted or inbred litter.

It is a very simple procedure to castrate a male rabbit and involves only a very short anaesthetic taking just a few minutes. The female spay is more complex and is best undertaken by a vet experienced in rabbit surgery. We always advise speaking to several vets for their opinions, quotes and to enquire about their experience of operating on rabbits.

After castration, a mature adult can remain fertile for up to 4-5 weeks so please separate him from any females he might come into contact with. If a male is castrated immediately at puberty, i.e. his filled testicles appear then there is no need to separate him from females following his op.

Where this might be difficult, we have heard of innovative solutions such as wrapping both sexes in 'nappies' thus preventing any genital contact between the two partners. However, this is far from being a reliable form of rabbit contraception and, if there should be an unplanned accident, then it would be advisable to have both the boy and girl neutered immediately afterwards which will ensure the female doesn't have to go through an unwanted pregnancy.

Rabbit 'nappies' are *not* a reliable form of contraception!

Prevention of spraying

Castration will prevent a buck from spraying urine. However, please do not assume that un-neutered bucks are going to spray as this is certainly not the experience of all owners. Some bucks are trigger-happy sprayers and for these living as house-rabbits, castration isn't optional unless you want smelly urine staining your floors, walls and even ceilings.

If your buck is prone to spraying then you can ensure you avoid positioning his hutch at eye/hair level where a quick squirt can leave you drenched in smelly urine. One of ours has a special knack of aiming for human mouths so we have re-positioned his hutch at ground level where it is not a problem and his spraying has now ceased.

Prevention of uterine cancer

While there are few, if indeed any, *medical* advantages in castrating a buck, spaying a doe does have definite medical benefits.

Spaying will also prevent uterine cancer which is said to be fairly common in older rabbits. Some reports quote up to 80% of older does contracting the condition although this is not necessarily matched by the experience of Veterinary Surgeons or rabbit owners. However, this observation must be balanced by the fact that many asymptomatic uterine tumours probably pass un-noticed or a rabbit may die from another illness and it is only by having a Post Mortem examination that the condition is detected.

In addition to preventing uterine cancer, other benefits of spaying include:

- Prevention of excessive weight gain: unspayed and unbred does are prone to becoming overweight although even spayed females can also become fat without adequate daily exercise.
- Prevention/minimising of hormone-related behaviour such as stroppy or territorial behaviour and 'turfing' (see below)
- Easier litter-training
- Spaying will minimise or totally eradicate phantom pregnancies in does.

Once bred, females can become more stroppy and temperamental if breeding isn't repeated and some will develop a tendency to spray like males if they are not mated again. We would **never, ever** recommend that any owner 'lets her have a litter' for fun or in the mistaken belief that this is in her best interests or has any health benefits. It doesn't. It can also lead to unwanted behaviour in the future.

It is sometimes suggested that castration can lead to a longer life-expectancy but there are mixed views on this and these seem to relate largely to the lower risk of males being killed through fighting, rather than castration itself conferring any health benefits.

Before you make your decision, the risks and benefits must be considered so that you can make an informed and confident decision. If you are uncertain whether to proceed, then please discuss this with your rabbit-savvy vet. At the same time, also ask how many spaying operations he/she undertakes and whether there have been any complications. Your vet's experience may help you make the best decision for your rabbit. Please ensure you choose a vet who is experienced in treating and operating on rabbits. Remember, any surgical risk is subject to three factors:

- the health and condition of the patient

- the anaesthetic used and the competence of the person administering it
- the surgery itself and whether there are any unforeseen complications
- and the latter two can depend on the skills, experience and competence of those involved in undertaking the surgery.

Spaying of French Lops and giant breeds can be a little more controversial amongst some rabbit owners using the once-valid argument that uterine cancer is more common in rabbits aged over 4-5 years which, a few decades ago, matched the average life expectancy of larger breed rabbit. Years ago there was some truth to this but thanks to improved lifestyles, diets and veterinary care, large breed life expectancies can now be very much longer. A growing number of ours have celebrated their 10th birthdays and overall life expectancy of our French Lops is now around 7-8 years with our eldest reaching 10.5 years.

This uterine tumour, the size more commonly found in a dog, was removed from an otherwise healthy 4 year old French Lop doe retired from breeding.

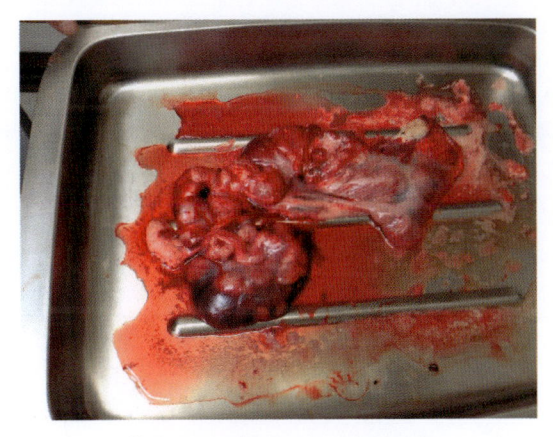

Large uterine cancer tumour
Photo: courtesy of P Halkyard

Behavioural reasons

Neutering can have benefits for owners who want to litter-train their rabbits.

During the main breeding season, there can be a temporary breakdown in litter-training, with bucks beginning to spray while both males and females might deposit their droppings outside their tray as they territorially mark 'their space'.

If you have a sexually-frustrated buck, then you might find he starts circling your ankles, mounting your arms and legs and trying to mate with shoes, cushions, brooms, soft toys - anything he can. Usually males display this sexual behaviour towards adult female hormones and can undoubtedly tell the difference between a male or female human owner.

As for females, un-spayed females can become quite stroppy and begin to fling their food bowls or litter tray around and become quite grumpy. These 'problems' are likely to worsen significantly once she has been bred.

Turfing

Females can also be extremely messy in their hutches: digging in their food bowls, kicking litter out of litter trays and piling it all together into a messy heap in the centre of their hutch. Previously-bred females are then likely to spray their newly created mound, along with their hutch walls, adding a strong urine odour to their dishevelled hutch and this takes only a few minutes following cleaning out!. This activity is known as 'turfing' and is probably intended, by a fertile and frisky female, to attract the attentions of a mate.

Neutering can resolve these potential problems - however, they often simply pass naturally in time and your bun will return to his/her docile self, sprawled out on your lounge floor craving fuss and attention.

Again, as stated earlier, it is never advisable for try to resolve a female rabbit's natural mating instincts by taking the view *"Oh, I'll just let her have a litter to be kind to her"*. In practice, this is much more likely to worsen the situation and can be highly irresponsible if you are unable to offer the time commitment necessary, or if the rabbits do not have good homes to go. We believe it is far more responsible to take a pro-active approach and have your rabbit neutered.

Bonding Rabbits

above: 3 generations of a French Lop family

Rabbits are social animals and love to have rabbit-company, especially if they live outdoors in a large hutch.

Having one or more companions provides stimulation, and helps prevent boredom and it is very rewarding for you to watch your rabbits interact, snuggle up together, mutually groom and generally play together. As a general observation, rabbits living in compatible pairs or small groups appear much happier than those housed singly.

A pair of bonded Netherland Dwarf rabbits

If you are about to adopt a young rabbit now, please consider adopting not just one but 2 or even 3 because this is the easiest way to ensure they'll all get along together in the longer-term.

Introducing rabbits at a later date usually involves having to go through a process of bonding them together - although this is not always the case. Much depends on the individual rabbits themselves, their personalities and the way they've been reared and handled.

If you are uncertain about adopting more than one rabbit at the moment but think you might like more in the future, then we strongly recommend you adopt a boy first as it is usually very easy to introduce a girl later (once he's had 'the snip'!).

A Group of Rabbits:

The ideal scenario would be to adopt 2-3 littermates which will ensure you are already buying a 'bonded' couple/group. If this is not possible, then you can usually simply introduce youngsters of the same or similar age from the same breeder, at the same time. By adopting from the same breeder, you are less likely to take infection risks, as you can when adopting from different breeders/centres. Every rabbit will be carrying certain bacteria but when rabbits from different breeders meet, each will probably be carrying different bacteria which increases the risk of potential infection since baby rabbits can have quite immature immune systems.

If you already have one rabbit and would like to find him/her a companion, then the success or otherwise of this can be determined by a number of factors:

- **What is the age of your present rabbit?** It is usually extremely easy to introduce youngsters before they reach puberty. After puberty, rabbits can be more territorial and aggressive towards the arrival of a new rabbit. However, this varies greatly between different rabbits.

- **Is your present rabbit male or female?** It is nearly always easier to introduce a girl to a boy than the other way around.

Female rabbits will usually live happily together providing they are *introduced gradually on neutral territory* which is especially important for older rabbits. Young females introduced at a young age, soon after weaning, generally get on well together immediately while two female litter-mates could prove the ideal pair. Females living together will probably need to be spayed at puberty to minimise hormonal territorial behaviour which can lead to fighting.

Females (i.e. adult females) tend to be much more territorial and might not welcome a new rabbit sharing their space - although some love to have a hutch-mate and will give a new arrival a quick sniff then return to her food bowl.

If your present rabbit is a boy, then he will probably welcome the arrival of a pretty girl-friend with open paws and obvious delight. Castration is essential in any boy rabbits in order to prevent breeding if paired with a girl, and to reduce the risks of fighting if paired with a boy although this is a combination we advise against.

Introducing two adult males is asking for trouble as they will almost certainly fight aggressively. The only way two adult males can usually live together is to have them both castrated. However, two littermates or males introduced as youngsters who are then never separated, will sometimes live happily together, but castration might be required in the future should any fighting occur and even then there are no guarantees of harmony.

- **Is your present rabbit neutered?** If you have a boy, then it is **essential** that he is castrated to prevent unplanned pregnancy. A boy can mature as early as 10 weeks so it is vital you keep a close watch on his gentlebun department and as soon as his testicles descend, it is time to book his appointment with the vet who will usually give him a free check to confirm he's ready for his 'snip' prior to booking his surgery.

If you have an adult male, rather than a 'pubescent' adolescent, then you will need to wait about 4-5 weeks following castration before introducing a girl-friend. Adult males can still be fertile for several weeks after their op so precautions must be taken.

Unspayed females can be especially territorial and it is usual beneficial to have them spayed before introducing a new friend.

- **What is your present rabbit's temperament?** Try to find a rabbit with a temperament which will complement, i.e. don't put two aggressive rabbits together but aim to have one who is more dominant than the other. This might read as unfair but, in practice, one rabbit is often more dominant than the other, just like in the natural Rabbit Kingdom in the wild.

- **Have you had a recent rabbit-bereavement?** If your rabbit was used to having a companion around and he/she dies, then the surviving rabbit can pine quite markedly. In a worst-case scenario, the pining and stress of this can be so severe that he/she will stop eating and this can lead to gastric stasis setting in which can be a potentially fatal condition in itself.

In a more typical case, your surviving rabbit will just look thoroughly miserable and dejected. Please observe him/her closely to ensure he/she doesn't succumb to any infections which his/her late-companion might have suffered from and give lots of extra fuss, favourite foods, treats and favourite toys etc. as a distraction. Usually, the pining will start to decline after about a week or so but your rabbit will probably be very receptive to having a new friend.

If your rabbit died due to an infection, please ensure your own rabbit isn't at risk or showing any symptoms prior to introducing a new friend. We recommend waiting 2-4 weeks which is the longest incubation period for most rabbit diseases.

Introducing a New Rabbit

To introduce a new rabbit, we recommend the following steps:

1. With your new rabbit watching, snuggle your present rabbit on your knee then put him/her down to watch while you then snuggle your new rabbit.

2. Now s**nuggle both rabbits together** on your knee and offer lots of nose-rubs and shoulder massages, whatever seems most popular and appreciated.

3. Sometimes, the two rabbits will bond in this way and stretch out together to enjoy more fuss.

If not:-

Please find a **neutral area** which your present rabbit/s have never been in such as an area of your garden, a garage, garden shed, bathroom, the bath, the back of your car i.e. anywhere which is unfamiliar and won't carry the scent of either rabbit.

Now, follow the snuggling-routine as above

Next, pop both rabbits down on the ground/floor together and watch. They will probably sniff at each other and your present rabbit might lunge at the new arrival. If so, push his/her nose to the ground/floor in a submissive posture and fuss both of them together. If your present rabbit is a boy, he will probably mount a girl which is normal, so just leave him assuming he has been castrated and isn't actually penetrating her or she isn't becoming distressed. Mounting by either rabbit and at either the head or tail end is normal for both sexes because the mounting is also an expression of dominance and not merely sexual.

If fighting persists, then please ensure the new rabbit doesn't become stressed. It might be better to try again tomorrow with a young, just-weaned rabbit rather than risk a stress-induced illness and the new rabbit becoming miserable or feeling under threat.

There are arguments for using both a large and small area for bondings. A large area more closely replicates their natural state in the wild and offers more space for each rabbit, space to 'escape' and is less likely to be an exclusive territory. However, a small space can sometimes be more functional for bondings as it allows you to intervene if necessary and also forces the rabbits to tolerate each other in a confined space. This is generally the option we would recommend but you also need to watch and learn from your rabbits to see which they respond most positively to, and act on this

Let them explore together. A little chasing is normal as they establish who is to be the dominant partner/pal. Let them do this or even pull a little fur. If there is fighting with biting, separate them immediately and try again later. Spraying the misbehaving rabbit lightly with a water bottle can help.

Once they're getting on together in the 'neutral area', offer a little more space and more snuggles together. Then, pop them together in their new home. This must have been thoroughly cleaned to remove as many traces of its previous occupant's scent and so smell as neutral as possible. Try to alter its position in the home or garden so that it becomes a 'new' cage/hutch/bed and its former occupant will be distracted a little by exploring his/her new surroundings.

Bonding can take patience with some rabbits but is always worthwhile and it's very rewarding and enjoyable to watch your rabbits snuggle contentedly together.

Often, the bonding is 'instant' and it isn't actually necessary to follow the tips given above and your rabbit will be much happier to have some rabbit-company. They can now live happily together *(remember to neuter, if necessary, of course),* share food bowls, bottles, litter tray, housing and bedding as fully-bonded companions.

Our bonding methods

In our experience, bonding has always been extremely easy and our rabbits live happily together as a group of up to 8 girls who play together daily then return to their 30' overnight hutches in groups of 2-3.

When we introduce a new rabbit we follow the same methods. Any new rabbit from an external source is always quarantined 30' away from our hutches for 4 weeks before being allowed to come into contact with our existing rabbits and we have them tested for E. Cuniculi and coccidiosis before allowing them on the grass or contact with any existing resident rabbit. This is a standard precaution just incase the new rabbit might be carrying any illnesses or infections plus it also allows time to get to know the new rabbit, judge his/her character and personality and we can observe that he/she is eating, drinking and passing normal droppings.

Once given a clean bill of health, for most rabbits we use a 3' square pen of about 3' height and place this in a 'neutral' area of the garden. After going through the snuggling routine, then we place the new rabbit in first for about 5-10 minutes whilst still snuggling the earlier rabbit. Then we pop in the existing rabbit. If there is any undue chasing then we reach over the top to push the bully's nose to the ground and let the other rabbit mount him/her in this position. This also has the effect of introducing the new rabbit's scent to the existing rabbit.

Generally, bondings take about 10-15 minutes but we closely watch and monitor behaviour over the following few hours incase there are any subsequent 'tiffs' which, occasionally, there are but harmony is very soon restored.

We are always cautious on the first night that a pair are together for the first time and do a few overnight checks. However, when bonding is carried out carefully, with understanding of the rabbits involved, their behaviour and feelings being paramount, then we find that bonding normally occurs quickly and tends to be permanent.

It's definitely worth investing a few hours to take the time to bond rabbits carefully – and the rewards are reaped when you see them flopped in a heap together enjoying a mutual grooming session.

Pairing rabbits with guinea pigs?

A common question asked is can rabbits be paired with guinea pigs?

We do not recommend pairing rabbits with guinea pigs because the two animals are very different and it is far better for an animal to obtain companionship from its own species.

A rabbit can cause internal injuries to a guinea pig by treading on them while a powerful kick can have fatal consequences. In retaliation, a guinea-pig can give a rabbit a nasty nip which could develop into a serious abscess requiring surgery.

Also, the two species have very different environmental preferences, i.e. rabbits enjoy a cool climate whereas guinea-pig need warmth along with different dietary requirements which cannot be easily provided when they are sharing the same accommodation.

Introduction to rabbit-breeding

Please note: We feel breeding is most definitely not an activity to be entered into lightly, or casually, without assessing whether you have the knowledge and extensive time-commitment required – and permanent loving homes for the youngsters.

Before going ahead with breeding, always ask yourself:

- "Why do I want to breed my rabbits?"
- "What will I achieve through breeding?"
- "Are my rabbits of breeding quality with a full pedigree for both parents?"
- "Do I have the time commitment, knowledge and experience to proceed?"
- "Do I have homes for the offspring?"

It is surprisingly time-consuming to care for and monitor young babies and their mother, feeding throughout the day is required together with regular handling of the babies to ensure they are used to human contact.

It is never a good idea to 'let her have just one litter' for 'fun' as you will probably find your sweet-natured rabbit-girl becomes a stroppy, hormone-fuelled terror following breeding. Spraying is quite common and you'll probably find she digs increasingly in her food bowl, combining it with the contents of her litter tray all of which will probably become a proudly-produced mound in the centre of her hutch/cage and then lovingly sprayed with smelly urine, behaviour known as 'turfing'. Immediately following cleaning, disinfecting and a general 'freshen up', it will take her a mere 5 minutes to repeat her paw-work once her soiled food and bedding have been replaced. Hence we never recommend casual breeding and allowing 'just one litter' holds no health or psychological benefits for her. So, for her sake and yours, please don't!

Suitable parents?

Before even considering breeding, look at the rabbits you have including their body shape, head shape and ensure there are no faults such as maloccluded jaws, molar spurs or even runny eyes, since these animals should never be bred. Always mate together two rabbits who compliment each other so that if the male has a slightly narrower head this could be corrected by mating him with a female with the features he lacks.

Compatible colours?

Also, colour must also be considered since not all colours are compatible with each other. It's a good idea to obtain a pedigree or a colour ancestry of their parents from their breeder so that you can choose which rabbits are going to be most compatible and produce the colours you are aiming for or hoping to improve by producing the litter. Via even a basic knowledge of colour genetics which is beyond the scope of this companion care guide, it is possible to work out exactly which colour genes the parents are carrying and then, using this knowledge and experience, work on improving your rabbit.

Mating and Fertility cycle

Female rabbits have two uterine horns and two separate cervices. Some rabbit breeders have reported simultaneous pregnancies with unrelated litters being carried in each of the uteri, although to the best of our knowledge, this has never been conclusively proven, nor has it been proven otherwise. Unlike other species, rabbits do not 'come into season' or show any signs of bleeding. Instead, they have a fertility cycle but are 'induced ovulators' meaning that the process of mating will stimulate ovulation.

Once the prospective parents are selected then it's time to plan the mating. Unlike most mammals, female rabbits do not have an immediately obvious fertility cycle or visibly come into season so close observation is required to reveal when she is most likely to be receptive. If you run your hand along her back and her tail jerks up like a brazen little hussie, then this is a fairly reliable sign.

Females tend to be territorial in their hutches/cages so it is better to take her to her suitor on his territory where she will almost certainly be eagerly welcomed. Another way is to pop both rabbits together in a safe, enclosed garden and let them run circles around each other, running, binkying, chasing and mounting just like their wild relatives. This also gives both prospective parents the option of an unforced mating. The buck is also likely to spray the does with a well-aimed jet of urine. Nice!

The mating itself is likely to be over very quickly. The circling and 'dancing' will culminate in the buck mounting the doe, hopefully but not necessarily, at the correct end, giving a few thrusts then falling off her with a satisfied grunt while she remains in situ, possibly looking a bit startled by the whole thing. It can take a few moments for him to recover and then he'll probably stand at her side thumping loudly to proudly broadcast what a successful, willing and able stud he is.

If the mating was successful then this will trigger ovulation. After 14-18 days, it is sometimes possible to very carefully and very gently palpate the proud mum-to-be and feel the new family now about the size and shape of small olives.

Palpating a pregnancy

To do this, place the mum-to-be on a flat surface with her facing you and then very gently feel her right side by sliding your upturned hand beneath her tummy. Gently bring your thumb and forefinger together as you feel upwards with your fingers while pressing lightly in from her side with your thumb. If she is pregnant then you should be able to feel grape-sized embryos between your thumb and fingers. Please, only attempt this is you are confident. If you are apprehensive about doing this for fear of harming the embryos, then it's best to ask an experienced breeder or rabbit-savvy veterinary surgeon for advice and a demonstration.

A successful palpation will confirm your rabbit is pregnant and you can then begin to prepare for the arrival of the new family of 1-6 or more kits following a gestation of approximately 31-33 days. However, if you are highly attuned to your rabbit's normal behaviour, you will spot the changes in her behaviour and mood and this itself can almost confirm the pregnancy. However, some pregnancies will be 'false' and culminate in a flurry of nest-building around day 18 following which the doe is likely to sit expectantly in her nest looking grouchy. A few days later it will be forgotten and the nest abandoned.

Nesting

Sometimes nest-building will start mid-way through the pregnancy although occasionally, some mums will begin plucking fluff and rearranging their bedding as early as day 3. Others won't show any signs until just 20 minutes before birth when there will be a frantic nest-building session followed by fluff-plucking from her belly. A few mums won't build a nest at all so then you will have to help out and make one for her using her fur once she's delivered and the litter are fed and settled. It's a good idea to keep a 'fur bag' from grooming sessions for such purposes so you can use her own familiar fur.

If any kits chill in the meantime, pick up mum's scent by rubbing your hands on her or in her litter tray, then warm them up in your hand and pop them into the nest. Then check it regularly. In the case of a small litter or babies who aren't retaining their body heat, microwaveable heat pads, such as the pink plastic discs produced by SnuggleSafe, can provide up to 5-6 hours gentle warmth for young babies while also being useful for convalescing rabbits *(they're handy hot water bottle alternatives for humans too)*.

Delivery

Delivery takes around 15-20 minutes and mum will/(should!) feed her newborn immediately after washing them, gently nosing them towards her 8 teats.

A nest of newborn

The young are born bald and are very susceptible to chilling until their nest coat grows so it is essential to check the nest regularly to ensure there are no strays. Any stillborn babies are usually delivered outside the nest and should be removed later in the day when both mum and her new family are settled.

If they're living together, the proud (or smug!) father **must always be separated** from the mother several days **before** she is due to give birth, to prevent mating immediately after birth or before the newborn are even weaned. Although such intensive breeding may occur in the wild, this is not recommended since it would lead to premature weaning of the earlier litter and be extremely draining on the mother leading to potential health problems.

Baby rabbits are usually fed 2-6 times daily. Many textbooks suggest there is just one daily feed but in our 45+ years experience, we have never found this to be the case and our mums tend to feed much more frequently, usually around 2am, 6am, 10am and a few more feeds during the day at less regular times.

Normally our girls are out in their pens during the daytime but when a mum has a new litter we leave her undisturbed with her family for the first 3 days then she will join her friends in their shared pens for a few hours in the morning and afternoon, being returned for a few hours in-between so she can nurse her family if she wishes.

Once the kits have left the nest, some will follow their mother around trying to feed throughout the day and appearing to constantly crave milk. The mother will stand over her young on stretched legs and the young will suckle lying on their backs, kicking with their rear legs. Whilst feeding, the mother will lick their genitals to stimulate elimination. After about 5-10 minutes, she will leave the nest, clean her teats and, hopefully, cover the nest again if the young have not yet grown their coats. If she doesn't, then cover it yourself to keep the babies warm and check they are all still in the nest and plump and that no babies have been dragged out whilst still attached to her teats. If there are any strays, warm them and replace them deep in the nest.

Any which have missed 2 feeds from mum must be fed by their breeder before they weaken. Hold the mother on her back and hold the baby to her nipples and s/he should suckle greedily. Just-fed young babies will have large abdomens visibly full of milk. When hungry, they can often be heard 'crying' for their mother or can stray from their nest in search of milk.

Just-fed kit with visible milk line

The young are born blind, deaf and without fur, barely resembling rabbits at all. However, rabbit milk is very rich and over the next two weeks they will grow rapidly in size, grow a fur coat, open their eyes and gradually start to explore the nest from about 18 days old. Whilst suckling, it is important to give the mother as much quality food as she will eat and an ample supply of clean, fresh water as lactating does are very thirsty.

Sleepy young kits in their nest

The young are weaned at approximately 6 weeks, occasionally sooner or, sometimes, longer. The larger rabbits can be removed from their mother earlier, allowing their smaller siblings to have a greater share of milk/food and catch up with their bigger brothers and sisters. Always remove mum from the babies and let the youngsters grow accustomed to her not being around.

Occasionally, it is necessary to hand-rear a litter offering feeds, ideally feeing the kits from mum whenever possible or, should the kits become orphaned, syringe-feeding using full-fat goats' milk which can take 1-2 hours every 4-6 hours **day and night** for up to 3-4 weeks and involves a huge round-the-clock time commitment. However, it can be extremely rewarding to watch a litter progress and develop and then move to a new home with new owners, if you can bear to part with them, that is, who keep you informed of their progress throughout their rabbit's life. A responsible breeder is always very selective about the sort of person whom they'll allow to adopt their babies and will always take the time and trouble to offer advice prior to and following adoption usually for the life of the baby. If the prospective adopter is a first-time rabbit owner then care information must be provided. Please do not give the youngsters to a pet shop chain to resell.

Hand-rearing baby rabbits

Breeding is not always straight-forward and does not always progress as hoped. Litters can be neglected, attacked, scattered, trampled or can chill rapidly if they crawl outside of their the nest or are accidentally dragged out following a feed. Some will simply fail to thrive and, in order to save them, it's down to you to play 'mum' and hand rear them.

If the mother is alive and has plenty milk, the best option is to feed the babies from her. Lay her on her back and cradle her in your arms. Then introduce the babies onto her belly and guide them to her nipples to suckle.

Feeding kits from an inexperienced mum!

If the babies are orphaned then they can be fostered by another mother with a litter of approximately the same age providing the total number of babies is not going to be too large for the mother to rear. If this is likely, then you could foster some babies and hand-rear the rest.

We have successfully hand-reared many litters, right from 20 minutes after birth so it **is** worth doing, but you'll have your work cut out for the next few weeks, especially with larger-breeds and, sadly, it isn't always successful.

Young babies can have difficulty retaining their body heat – so adding a heat pad, which can provide 5-6 hours warmth, to their nest can significantly increases their survival chances, particularly for small litters or a single baby. It is best to have 2-3 heat pads, such as Snugglesafe heat pads, so that they can be easily switched when they begin to cool down.

Experience has shown us that bitch/kitten milk replacement formula such as Cimicat or Lactol are some of the best options. This should be made up to its maximum strength using boiled, cooled (but still warm – aim for just above human body temperature) water and fed using sterilised syringes, or a dropper for newborn babies. Alternatively, full-fat goats' milk can be easier to use, produces excellent results and does not need diluting. This is available from most supermarkets.

Syringe-feeding goats' milk to a very hungry and co-operative orphan who strongly sucked milk from the syringe

- Always aim the syringe to the side of the mouth and never towards the back of the throat since this can lead to fatal aspiration of the syringe's contents.

- Feed until the belly looks full. We do this every 4-6 hours day and night. It is time consuming but it does give the best results.
- After any feed, always stimulate the genital area to encourage urination and defecation. Formula milk can be sticky so it's best to gently wipe any dribbles immediately using a piece of cotton wool dampened in warm water. After drying the babies, return them to their nest and check them regularly to ensure there are no strays.
- A probiotic, such as AviPro or Protexin will benefit their digestive systems after 3 weeks of age.
- Once the babies start to nibble on solid food, ensure there is a good supply of clean, fresh hay together with quality, nutritious pellets available, but no veggies which are likely to cause tummy upsets in young rabbits.
- When the babies reach 4-5 weeks, the regular syringe feeds can be gradually reduced, starting with the larger babies first, so that by 6 weeks of age they are eating only solid food.

Above: full, tight belly with visible milk:

A word of warning
- you probably won't be able to part with any of the litter!

Showing or Exhibiting Rabbits

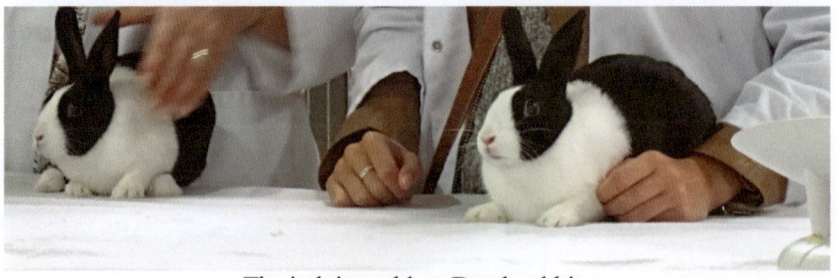

The judging table – Dutch rabbits

Showing or exhibiting rabbits can be a controversial subject amongst companion pet owners but it is a recognised hobby amongst enthusiasts. Rabbit shows are where you are most likely to see some of the best quality, perfectly marked and patterned rabbits along with a wide variety of common, popular and rare breeds, so a brief overview has been included here for those readers who are interesting in learning more about what showing involves.

Rex – awaiting judging

UK rabbit breeders aim to produce 'perfect' rabbits which meet the strict breed standards stipulated by the British Rabbit Council (BRC). The rabbits are taken to shows held around the country where they are formally judged and the best in class will be awarded a prize, usually with additional prizes for the two runners-up. Some shows might also stage a 'pet' section where rabbits are judged on their overall condition, health, fitness etc. rather than their conformity to a breed standard. This can form an introduction to showing for pet owners.

Traditionally showing rabbits was seen as the hobby of middle-aged working class men donning white coats and peaked caps breeding 'perfect' rabbits. Equally traditionally, these would be housed in undersized hutches, often only 2' square or 3' x 2', in a shed in the foot of the garden and any rabbits bred which 'didn't make the grade might be 'culled' which could mean killed, eaten or sold on as pets. Thankfully this is a very old view and showing rabbits today is very different to 50 years ago. Standards have improved so much that ongoing positive changes are seen on an almost annual basis at some of the larger shows.

Netherland Dwarf in show pen

While awaiting judging, rabbits will be housed usually in small wired cube partitions, taken out by their owners for 'preparation' which includes grooming glossy coats to get the best possible shine and checking their own personal exhibits are in the best condition visually. Show rabbits are generally spotless with perfectly groomed coats, bright eyes and perfect pedicures. There will be no muddy paws, soiled sticky bottoms and most definitely no maloccluded jaws. Show rabbits are bred for perfection, or as close to perfection as possible, and shows will feature the 'pride and joy' of their proud breeders.

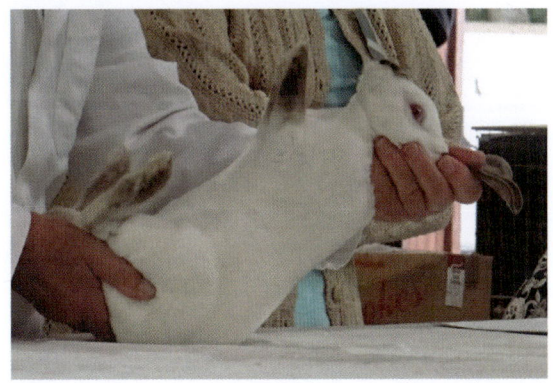

Judging – to match British Rabbit Council Breed Standards

Judging

Judging involves examining each rabbit within a particular class closely. They will be weighed, visually checked all over, coats examined for any faults which can include stray hairs, slightly imperfect markings, wrongly coloured toe nails or other deviations from the Breed Standards and then the top one to three in each class will be awarded a prize rosette and sometimes a small prize which is usually little more than the entry fee. There is no money to be made in showing. It is done for pride and enjoyment, not financial reward.

Sought-after trophies

Showing has been criticised by some pet owners in the past, perhaps not without due cause, but showing has moved on a long way in the last few decades and standards continue to improve, so it is only fair to give a balanced view.

Just 15-20 years ago, it would be almost unusual for rabbits to have so much as a water bottle in their show-pens prior to judging. Today they have not only water but hay which not so long ago was unthinkable. Battery-powered fans are often to keep them cool in hot weather and some breeders add toys or hay stuffed into cardboard rolls for their rabbit's amusement or even supply fresh hand-picked grass brought from home. This also reflects the changing and vastly improved welfare standards along with a newer younger generation entering the hobby, also known as 'the fancy'.

These rabbits are often cared for as pets rather than 'stock', are allowed to run around and dig in their owner's garden, pop inside their owner's homes etc. and are a world apart from the old 'traditional' show rabbit forced to sit in a square show pen or undersized hutch at home.

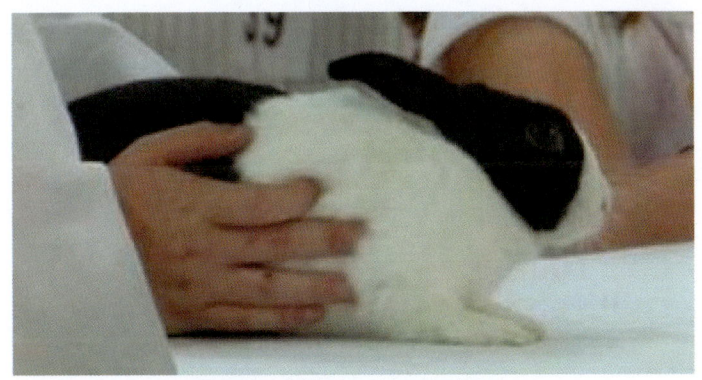

Dutch rabbit awaiting judging

If you are interested in showing rabbits then you will need to become a member of the British Rabbit Council and, of course, have rabbits of a showable standard matching the Breed Standards, available from the BRC.

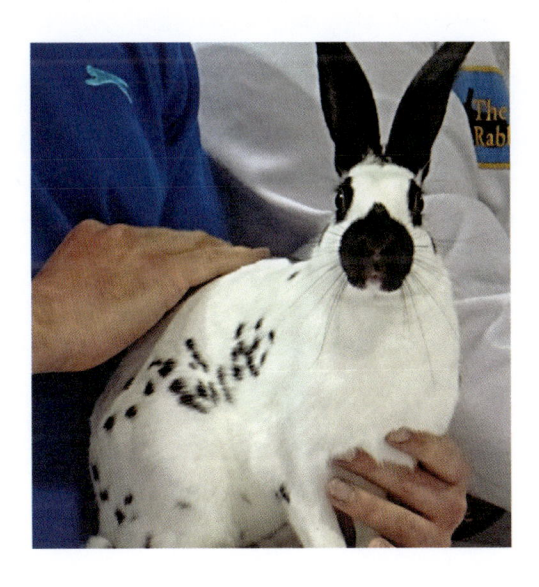

Rabbit Health

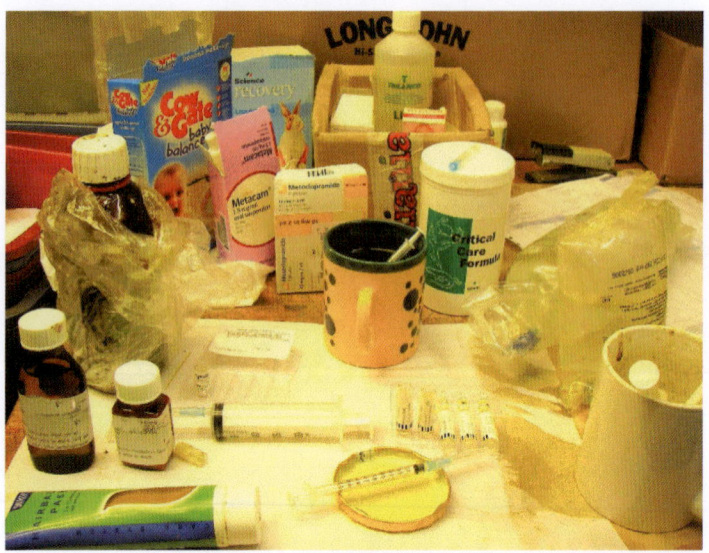

A typical first aid kit in use!

Disclaimer: *These pages deliberately aim to provide very basic information only and are not intended as a substitute for qualified veterinary advice, care or treatment. The conditions described on these pages are not diagnostic of readers' own rabbits' conditions and treatments included here are for guidance only. The author accepts no liability for readers' rabbits and urges any reader to always seek a professional medical diagnosis and advice from a rabbit-savvy veterinary surgeon if you have any concerns about the health of your rabbits.*

Rabbits are generally healthy and hardy animals but they can also deteriorate rapidly should they become ill and, as prey animals, they often won't display obvious signs or symptoms of illness until any illness is quite advanced. Therefore, it is vital you are highly vigilant in checking your rabbit.

Look for signs of:

Behavioural changes -
- sitting quietly in a corner
- sitting apart from your other rabbits
- ignoring favourite toys
- sitting huddled up or grinding teeth which can be a sign of pain
- not rushing to the food bowl at feeding times
- refusing favourite treats

Signs of possible illness-
- a decrease in the amount of feed and water consumed
- reduction in number and size of droppings (can indicate **Gastric Stasis**)
- dehydration
- cold ears
- rapid breathing
- Sneezing or coughing (could be simple allergy or dusty-irritant, or **Pasteurella**)
- obvious abdominal tenderness
- bloated abdomen (could indicate **Gastric Stasis**)
- diarrhoea (rehydration may be necessary)
- poor coat quality, weight loss
- obvious weakness or splayed legs
- runny eyes or a white eye discharge (possible conjunctivitis or **Pasteurella**)
- dehydration
- purple tinge to lips, tongue (can indicate respiratory disease)
- breathing through the mouth rather than the nose

This is only a very brief summary and, if you have the slightest suspicion that your rabbit might be ill, then it is essential that he/she is examined by a **rabbit-savvy** veterinary surgeon without delay. Please note the contact details of your nearest rabbit-savvy vet **now** so that they are always immediately to hand incase needed urgently.

Rabbits usually live for 6-8 years, on average. Small dwarf breeds tend to have a longer life-span while the larger breeds, such as French

Lops, used to have a disappointingly shorter average life expectancy of about 4-5 years, although ours are now reaching 10 years and beyond which we are very proud of. However, husbandry, diet and healthcare factors can have a further influence on life-expectancy and prompt diagnosis of any medical conditions can ensure any illnesses don't rapidly develop to become fatal.

The most common problems include overgrown nails which should be regularly checked, overgrown teeth and gastro-intestinal disorders such as gastric stasis. If your rabbit develops any suspicious symptoms, runny eyes or nose (see **Pasteurella**), has a poor coat, sits alone huddled in a corner of the hutch, becomes lethargic, loses his/her appetite or appears to be losing weight then veterinary attention must be sought immediately.

If your young rabbit appears to be off its food, producing no droppings at all, is dehydrated and/or has a hard and lumpy, or very bloated abdomen, this can indicate mucoid enteropathy in a weanling or **Gastric Stasis** which requires immediate urgent treatment from a rabbit-savvy vet. The sooner this is treated then the greater the chances of recovery from this disease, known as the 'silent killer'. A rabbit suffering from stasis will need several days of intensive nursing round-the-clock - but s/he can recover if treated promptly.

Rabbits are considered 'exotic' pets by many vets and not all vets are used to treating rabbits. It is important to choose a vet who is familiar with rabbits, used to administering anaesthetics, performing routine spays and castrations and is confident with rabbits. Some vets are more comfortable with cats and dogs, others specialise in cattle, sheep or horses. It is worth contacting several surgeries or seeking a personal recommendation from another rabbit owner to ensure you choose the most suitable vet. One day your rabbit's life might depend on it.

Rabbit Health insurance

Although rabbits are generally healthy animals, if they become ill then vet fees can quickly mount up.

Illnesses or accidents can be unpredictable with equally unpredictable bills to match. Fortunately, pet insurance is available from companies such as PetPlan and Exotics Direct and for a monthly premium you can guard against such unexpected high bills knowing you will only need to pay the policy excess which is usually around £40-50.

We are often asked if having insurance is worthwhile. If your rabbit has one mild illness or needs a single, relatively minor treatment for a condition such as mites, then insurance is probably not worthwhile. However, if your rabbit needs several treatments per year then the premiums will probably be balanced out. But if your rabbit should require surgery e.g. for an abscess, broken limb or needs treatment for a more complex condition then this can easily reach 4-figures making the necessary treatment affordable.

Before taking out any policy, always ensure you obtain a quotation for the premiums and ensure the cover matches your needs. Check for any exclusions and read the small print particularly those relating to ongoing dental problems which your policy might exclude.

Any pre-existing medical conditions must be declared before taking out the policy and are likely to be excluded.

Insurers:

Exotics Direct: https://www.exoticdirect.co.uk

Pet Plan: https://www.petplan.co.uk/pet-insurance/rabbit-insurance/

Alternatively, your local vet surgery might offer its own scheme but before signing up, always ensure the vets are rabbit-savvy because some are not.

Abscesses

Any cut or wound puncturing the skin has the potential to form an abscess so always ensure any wounds are carefully cleaned and observed closely until fully-healed. It doesn't take much and even just a minor nip, an ingrained grass seed or small wood splinter can result in an abscess. Other facial and jaw abscesses can be caused by dental disease.

Abscesses beneath the skin are usually caused by Pasteurella multocida or staphylococcus aureus and can lead to swelling which can be most painful for the rabbit. Pasteurella can live within the nasal cavity and be spread via grooming either the rabbit's own body or his companion's.

Abscesses fill with a very thick pus with a toothpaste-like consistency and can be difficult to treat.

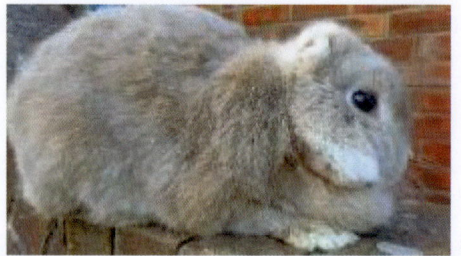

Earless dwarf lop with abscess on side of face

The abscess is about 30mm long and 15mm deep

Abscess treatment

Treatment varies according to the size of the abscess and whether it erupts and discharges pus outside the body or, subsides naturally. The vast majority will require veterinary treatment which can involve surgically removing the abscess and its enclosing capsule to prevent recurrence. If it subsides naturally, then it is likely to return. Some abscesses can grow very large i.e. up to, and occasionally larger than, the size of a hen's egg.

The first signs of an abscess are felt as a hard lump beneath the skin which feels tight over the swelling. As the abscess reaches the surfaces of the skin, it becomes more visible then, if left, can burst through the skin producing a mass of thick, pungent smelling pus which needs to be drained out and the abscess wound flushed to ensure all of the pus is removed followed by a course of antibiotics.

Home treatment

Often wounds are left open for the owner to continue twice-daily using an antiseptic solution or saline but care has to be taken to ensure the rabbit doesn't ingest antiseptic which can lead to diarrhoea. Another option which is possibly easier for rabbit owners to handle at home, is to use clear honey such as Manuka honey, twice daily, both inside the empty abscess cavity and on the skin outside the wound, taking care to remove the solidified honey plug inside the cavity before applying more.

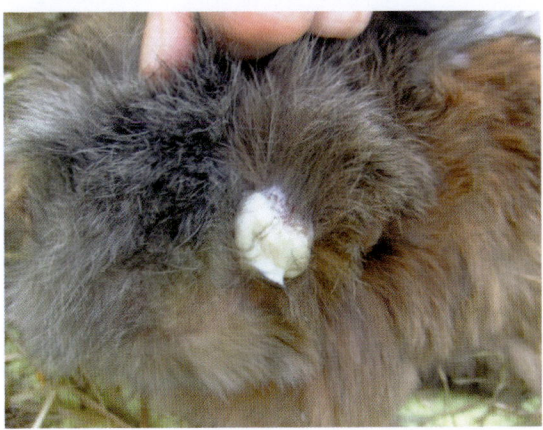

Thick pus draining from burst abscess

Some abscesses will need to be surgically removed to remove the pus and then rinsed with antibiotic solution or will have antibiotic beads impregnated with gentamycin inserted into the wound. The wound may be left open or partially open to enable it to drain naturally but will require bathing, to prevent further infection, as instructed by your vet.

However, some small and fully encapsulated abscesses seem to cause the rabbit no discomfort and the rabbit continues his normal life showing no signs of pain or irritation. In these cases, providing the remains small, they can be left untouched and undisturbed while still monitoring for any changes.

Progress of an erupting abscess

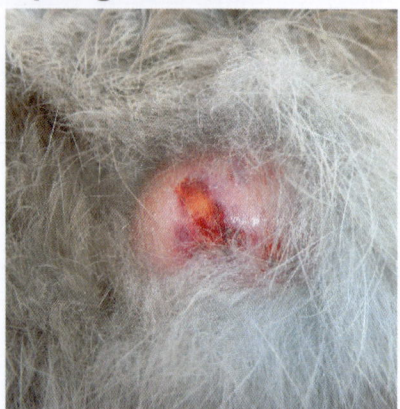

The abscess can be seen as it reaches the skin surface

The abscess bursts through the skin surface, in this case enclosed in its capsule, then releases a mass of pungent pus

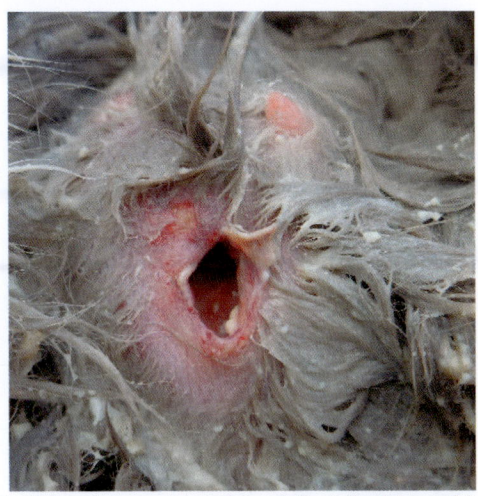

Following removal of the abscess capsule and first flushing which was followed by antibiotic treatment.

Digestive disorders

Overview

Stomach disorders are relatively common in rabbits of all ages, particularly youngsters under 12-14 weeks of age who tend to be prone to gastric upsets and mucoid enteropathy due to their sensitive young digestive systems. A change in droppings is often a first indication of stomach or gastro-intestinal disorder in adults who need urgent treatment. Youngsters and weanlings tend to sit hunched over, grinding their teeth in pain, passing few if any droppings or dollops of stringy yellow-brown mucus before invariably succumbing.

Rabbits produce mucus-coated pellets, known as 'caecotrophs', and normally eat them straight from their anus, a process known as caecotrophy. However, particularly if they are being fed a high-protein diet, they might leave these scattered on their hutch floor, or sit on them.

Normal rabbit droppings are hard, odourless and when closely examined, are highly fibrous. Caecotrophs are smelly mucus-coated pellets about 2-4cm long and can resemble a bunch of grapes.

Each are illustrated in the following photographs:

Above: Normal caecotroph pellet

Above: Normal healthy fibrous rabbit droppings

Above: A 'String of Pearls'. Rabbit is ingesting too much fur which is being excreted with the droppings which are passed strung together. Increase fibre in the diet and ensure your rabbit is groomed twice daily to help prevent excess fluff being swallowed

Coccidiosis

Coccidiosis is one of the most common infections amongst pet rabbits, particularly youngsters.

It is caused by a parasitic infection by Eimeria and there are 9 different species. One causes coccidiosis of the liver (hepatic coccidiosis) while the others cause intestinal symptoms (intestinal coccidiosis). The symptoms exhibited will vary depending upon which Eimeria parasite is responsible for the infection.

Typical symptoms include:
- retarded growth
- loss of appetite
- severe diarrhoea
- weakness
- death

The best prevention is strict hygiene, daily cleaning and ensuring droppings are removed before coccidia levels soar and also ensure droppings are not allowed to contaminate food. Some rabbit pellets contain a coccidiostat such as Robenidine or Coxiril® (diclazuril) as an aid in the prevention of coccidiosis. This is preventative treatment although this might be of dubious value because there is no guarantee that the rabbits are receiving the correct dosage and less effective drugs are used.

For confirmed coccidiosis, it is advisable for breeders to treat their entire stock with an effective and potent anti-coccidiostat such as Baycox every 6 months to keep any coccidia levels under control.

While adults can develop immunity to coccidiosis, youngsters can be quite susceptible to GI infections generally making preventative anti-coccidiostat treatment advisable at about 5-6 weeks of age.

A 'splat' from a rabbit with confirmed coccidiosis.
Similar faecal output can occur in other GI illnesses and only a veterinary examination can confirm the cause so rabbits with upset GI systems need urgent veterinary attention.

Diarrhoea

Rabbits can suffer from diarrhoea which can be infection-induced or caused by a simple change of diet or over-indulgence in veggies or fruits. In rabbits this can be serious and quickly lead to dehydration for which veterinary advice must be sought without delay.

If you see your rabbit with a slightly sticky, smelly bottom this might just be the result of sitting on sticky caecal pellets, which have the unfortunate habit of sticking to soft fluffy coats, rather than diarrhoea, which is liquid in consistency.

If your rabbit has diarrhoea, then there will be a very obviously 'runny bottom' and possibly liquid brown or greenish-yellow puddles, with a very strong unpleasant smell. Your rabbit is also likely to be very listless in appearance in a severe case and this requires instant veterinary attention.

Diarrhoea can be caused by
- Upset caused by dietary change
- Infection

Mild diarrhoea

Diarrhoea caused by a change of diet is easier to treat. In a mild case, if he/she is still eating and drinking and looks bright and perky, then we recommend withdrawing all mix and feeding only hay and water for 24-48 hours while monitoring your rabbit closely. If he/she becomes dehydrated, which is possible, then you will need to syringe-feed ground-up pellets mixed with warm water or a product such as Supreme Science Recovery solution which is ideal for a sick or recuperating rabbit while Critical Care solution is also good for emergency use. An adult rabbit with mild diarrhoea can also be treated by feeding with blackberry leaves which have astringent properties and can be found throughout the year growing wild in hedgerows. Wash them first and feed freely. Raspberry leaves have similar therapeutic benefits but are not so easily available. Leaves can be fed fresh or dried.

A simple basic test for dehydration is to pluck the loose skin over your rabbit's shoulders. Raise it a few centimetres and then release. It should instantly spring back but if it returns slowly or remains tented then this is a sign that your rabbit is already dehydrated and administering fluids now is essential.

Using a 5-10ml syringe, insert it behind the incisors and aim it towards the **side** of the mouth (never aim towards the throat since this can induce aspiration which can cause instant death) and very slowly squeeze 0.25–1ml into your rabbit's mouth. Wait for him to swallow and allow a few breaths then squeeze a little more and repeat. Never try to 'fill' your rabbit's mouth or squirt more until your rabbit has swallowed or you may risk aspiration.

If your rabbit is very resistant to this, please do not take any risks but take him/her along to your vet surgery where fluids can be given subcutaneously or intravenously. This is a safe, simple and stress-free way to quickly rehydrate an ill rabbit.

Severe diarrhoea

If your rabbit's diarrhoea is caused by infection or is profuse, then s/he will require immediate vet treatment. In a bad case, the diarrhoea will literally pour out of your rabbit like a slowly running tap and it might even be greenish/yellow in colour. If this is the case, then your rabbit will be feeling very miserable and will probably be quite lethargic and could rapidly dehydrate and deteriorate. Please take him to your vet for treatment with fluids and antibiotics. He/she might be admitted for observation and close monitoring.

Subcutaneous rehydration of ill rabbit

If your rabbit's coat becomes soiled then she/he will need to be bathed.

Diarrhoea and dietary change

Fruit and vegetables can be notorious for causing diarrhoea in youngsters who have not been weaned on these. Therefore it is important to introduce these very gradually. We recommend waiting until your rabbit is at least 12 weeks old and then introducing a little grass, waiting a day, then offering a little more and perhaps a dandelion leaf. Later you can move onto veg such as offering one slice of carrot and, assuming there are no adverse effects offer 2 slices after 48 hours and then gradually build up. The same principle can be applied when introducing other veg.

Diarrhoea caused by dietary change or an unofficial nibble on forbidden fruit or veg is very common in young rabbits. A sudden change of diet is never recommended and, if you must change your rabbit's feed, then please ensure any changes are gradual over a period of at least 10-14 days. One suggested regime for an adult would be to follow this programme:

Days 1-2, add 10% of the new feed to your rabbit's usual mix/pellets.

Days 3-4, add 20% of the new feed to your rabbit's usual mix/pellets.

Day 5-7, add 30% of the new feed to your rabbit's usual mix/pellets.

Day 8, add 40% of the new feed to your rabbit's usual mix/pellets.

Day 9, add 50% of the new feed to your rabbit's usual mix/pellets.

Day 10, add 60% of the new feed to your rabbit's usual mix/pellets.

Day 11, add 70% of the new feed to your rabbit's usual mix/pellets.

Day 12, add 80% of the new feed to your rabbit's usual mix/pellets.

Day 13, add 90% of the new feed to your rabbit's usual mix/pellets.

Day 14 onwards – rabbit will now be accustomed to the new diet.

Gastric Stasis

Caecotrophy

One of the main differences between rabbits and other mammals is their digestive system. A rabbit has a large caecum in which caecotrophs are produced from vegetable protein that is converted into mucus-coated, grape-like pellets, which are rich in bacterial protein. These 2-4cm long pellets are re-ingested immediately after being passed from the anus, a process known as caecotrophy.

If a rabbit is scattering these on the hutch floor, then it is probable that they are being fed an excessive amount of protein and the re-ingestion of caecotrophs can be encouraged by reducing the amount of pellets or mix fed and increasing hay consumption.

As a result of this digestive process, two different types of dropping are produced, mucus-coated caecotrophs (left) and normal, fibrous rabbit droppings (right):

This unique aspect of the rabbit's digestive system can also be the source of major health problems related to the digestive tract. Since caecotrophy is controlled by the adrenal glands and adrenalin is a stress hormone, stress must always be avoided in rabbits since stressful situations can adversely affect caecotroph production and this then leads to repercussions on the digestive process.

Another peculiarity associated with rabbits, is their inability to vomit. Whilst this holds many advantages, such as no risks of travel-sickness or aspiration of stomach contents associated with vomiting under general anaesthetic, it also has a major disadvantage: if a rabbit should develop a furball then, unlike cats who vomit them upwards for relief, your poor rabbit develops a blockage which can quickly develop into gastric stasis as the GI system shuts down and can become a potentially life-threatening condition.

In the straight-forward case of gastric stasis caused by stress, a furball or blockage, often the first pre-symptom is a reduction of droppings in his/her litter tray and these are likely to be much smaller and drier than normal. Occasionally there could be droppings mixed with mucus indicating the gut has slowed down. All these signs should set alarm bells ringing. Loudly.

An unhealthy mix of droppings and intestinal mucus

Rabbits are very susceptible to stress and their bodies, and the process of caecotrophy, respond to this with their digestive system shutting down due to excess adrenaline being produced. Therefore, always minimise any stresses to your rabbit.

If you notice that a food bowl has barely been touched or the droppings are reducing in size or number, seek advice **immediately**. At this stage, prompt treatment can save your rabbit's life.

The next symptom can be dehydration which can progress rapidly in warm/hot weather. Due to the blockage or static gut, your rabbit loses his/her appetite, feels bloated and stops drinking and this is the first noticeable symptom. To the inexperienced rabbit-keeper, the coat feels like that of a soft stuffed toy and if you pinch the scruff, it will remain tented rather than instantly spring back into place as it should do. By this stage, dehydration can be advanced but, a vet can administer rehydration fluids much more effectively than via syringe-feeding, so please take your rabbit to the vet as soon as you spot any suspect symptoms.

In advanced cases of dehydration, it will be very difficult to find any loose skin to pinch at the scruff as it will appear to be 'clinging' to the rabbit's body which will probably now be quite hard, swollen and very bloated.

To help prevent stasis occurring, always feed large quantities of long fresh meadow hay, preferably from a fresh farm bale (not the stale pre-packed branded bags found in many pet shops). This can be supplemented by other high fibre products such as Spillers' ReadiGrass, Dengi HiFi, Burgess Forages or similar products. Feed adults fresh vegetables and grass and, during a moult, always pluck or comb away any shedding fur to prevent it being ingested. This grooming is required at least 1-2 times daily during a heavy moult. Fresh grass and leafy green veg can help keep the stomach contents moist so we recommend feeding daily grass and some fresh leafy green veggies or dandelion leaves to rabbits prone to stasis.

It is essential for your rabbit's health that you consult a rabbit-savvy vet for treatment for stasis. It is better to always be prepared for an attack and have already made contact with local vets to determine who will be the best to treat your rabbit if ever urgent veterinary care is required. Having a rabbit-savvy vet close by is invaluable in rabbit-emergencies such as these.

Vet visit checklist - examination

The veterinary examination, by a rabbit-savvy veterinary surgeon, should include:
1. Temperature-taking to check for signs of infection (raised temperature) or advanced stasis (lower temperature).
2. The teeth must be examined incase the rabbit has overgrown molars (spurs) which are sharply cutting into the sides of his mouth and making eating painful or there could be other mouth injuries including something as simple as a stuck grass seed.
3. A careful and gentle palpation of the gut to feel for any blockages. An X-ray might also be taken.
4. The gut should be listened to using a stethoscope to determine whether it has reached a standstill and whether there is any trapped wind bubbling internally and uncomfortably.
5. Hydration should be tested.

Vet visit checklist - treatment

Your rabbit-savvy vet will probably recommend a course of treatment including:

- X-Ray to determine whether there is a blockage
- Providing IV or sub-cutaneous fluids
- Providing a motility stimulant such as metoclopramide and ranitidine* (given 2 hours apart to allow for the ranitidine to be absorbed)
- Providing simethicone to help disperse trapped wind.
- Providing pain relief using analgesia such as Metacam or Vetergesic
- Providing antibiotics by mouth to prevent overgrowth of clostridia
- Replacing gut flora via probiotic such as AviPro or Protexin
- Protexin Fibreplex, a prebiotic-rich, carrot-flavour paste containing 34% dietary fibre in a graduated syringe for easy administration, available in 15ml syringes with a recommended dosage of 1ml per kg of body weight three times daily
- Possible stomach-tubing to ensure your rabbit has some nutrition and fibre passing through

Please note: If you are inexperienced in treating stasis or do not feel confident in providing intensive nursing care yourself, it is often advisable to request hospitalisation in order to provide the best chance of recovery. A rabbit with gastric stasis often requires round-the-clock feeding, tummy rubs and intensive nursing care which sometimes can only practically be provided by a vet surgery.

In addition to the above, we home-treat uncomplicated cases of gastric stasis with a combination of:

- While still at the 'sluggish gut' stage: offering greens including dandelions, dandelion leaves, parsley, grass, curly kale, mint, small pieces of apple, banana i.e. anything 'wet' (to help increase hydration in the gut and to hydrate any blockage) and high-fibre feeds such as grass, hay and forage.

- syringe-feeding (e.g. vegetarian baby food or crushed pellets mixed into a pulp with water and pro-biotic) to ensure your rabbit gets some nutrition during the illness
- Pineapple juice (contains an enzyme, bromelain, which helps to break down the substance which binds fur together creating furballs). Pineapple chunks might also be helpful.
- Lots of water to restore hydration. Sometimes a rabbit will drink from a bowl when they refuse a bottle. If your rabbit isn't eating or drinking then syringe feeding water and a product such as Supreme Science Recovery Plus solution or Oxbow Critical Care is essential to provide electrolytes, fibre and sustenance during the period of treatment and recovery. Always aim the syringe towards the side of the mouth - never towards the throat as this can lead to accidental aspiration and death. Syringe water very slowly, 0.25- 0.5ml at a time and wait until your rabbit swallows and has taken 1-2 breaths before syringing any further fluid. It can be a good idea to flavour the water with pineapple juice or even Ribena to give it some taste and encourage your rabbit to swallow.
- Motility stimulants are important to keep the gut moving or try to re-start a gut which has shut-down. Suitable medications include Prepulsid (cisapride) which was the early drug of choice. However, this was withdrawn in 2000 due to cardiac side-effects in humans but was then relaunched with limited availability so may be difficult to source. Alternatively, and more easily available, Maxolon/metoclopramide, can be administered orally or by IV (intravenous) or SQ (subcutaneous) injection, but only if there isn't a blockage of the intestinal tract. Ranitidine can be given 2 hours before or after metoclopramide. Metoclopramide is not formally licensed for use in rabbits but is a useful motility stimulant and can be given either via injection or orally. An oral solution can be made by dissolving a 10mg tablet in 2ml water making a solution of 1mg per 0.2ml water. The dosage is 0.2ml/kg body-weight every 8 hours. We have also had some success in using Senna, a laxative which works by stimulating the lower gut but all motility stimulant drugs **must always be used with extreme care and only under veterinary supervision**. An X-ray may be required to diagnose this if any blockages cannot be felt via gentle palpation. If there is a blockage and motility stimulants are

administered, these could lead to an intestinal rupture **so a vet's professional opinion is essential.**

- Liquid paraffin is an old-fashioned method to help lubricate a dry gut or lubricate and help to shift a dried impaction. Some vets use this; others advise against it. An alternative can be malt paste used for cats with fur balls.
- Oral antibiotics are recommended for GI infections - and must be prescribed by a vet.
- Lectade is useful for oral rehydration. The powder is mixed with water and provides essential vitamins, minerals and electrolytes.
- Infacol (simethicone). This is available from the 'baby' counter at supermarkets or chemists, can help disperse uncomfortable gastro-intestinal wind.
- Gentle tummy-rubs can help ease pain, pass wind and seems to make the rabbit feel more comfortable. Don't be rough as your rabbit may already be in pain and have tender abdominal organs. Rough stimulation could lead to an internal rupture with fatal consequences.
- Heat pad (e.g. SunggleSafe) or hot water bottle wrapped in a towel to sit on, can be soothing.

* In an emergency...

A ranitidine solution can be made at home by crushing a 7.5mg tablet (available over the counter) and dissolving it in 5ml cooled boiled water. The dosage is 0.3-0.8ml for a 2.5kg rabbit; 0.6-1.6ml for a 5kg rabbit. Metoclopramide is available on prescription only. However, these drugs must not be given if there is any possibility your rabbit has a gastro-intestinal blockage because administration could lead to a gut rupture. An emergency simple oral rehydration solution can be made at home using one litre of cooled boiled water to which half a teaspoon of sea salt, a teaspoon of baking soda (not baking powder) and two teaspoons of sugar should be added.

In our experience, we have found that Supreme Recovery Solution is eagerly lapped up from a syringe, especially when mixed with warm water, not cold. It is pleasantly flavoured with aniseed and encourages ill rabbits to feed making syringe-feeding less of a struggle. With its high fibre content of 20%, electrolytes for rehydration and probiotic, it is perfect for rabbits suffering from gut disturbance and/or stasis and helps carry many through illness. It can also be used dry and sprinkled on food although we've used it mostly for syringe-feeding. Occasionally, the syringe may block and, if this happens, simply snip off part of the teat diagonally and continue to syringe slowly and carefully. Without the narrowed teat, there is less control over the amount being syringed so extra caution is needed

Many rabbits deteriorate rapidly and require round-the-clock intensive nursing, particularly during the first 3-4 days. Often a rabbit can appear to be a 'lost cause' and the owner may consider giving up. However, in our experience we sometimes find a rabbit will deteriorate and hit rock bottom and be at the point where we considering administering the last rites. Then, to our delight, some rabbits will unexpectedly surprise us by suddenly appearing slightly better then making a gradual recovery.

Treatment and full recovery takes about 8 days and usually on about the 5th day of treatment, there may be large quantities of clumpy droppings, sometimes coated in mucus, as gastric motility is resumed and the impacted caecum empties. These may have a foul smell and your rabbit might also pass some equally foul-smelling wind as s/he begins to recover.

The rabbit should then be fed grass, dandelions and hay to stimulate further gastric motility followed by their usual diet as your rabbit regains his/her lost weight. Pellets are normally introduced last of all but a little muesli type mix can be offered to aid the transition back onto their usual pellet diet.

Feeding a poor diet with inadequate fibre i.e. hay, grass and/or fresh vegetables, can encourage gastric stasis. Since caecotrophy is controlled by the adrenal glands and adrenalin is a stress hormone, stress must always be avoided in rabbits since stressful situations can adversely affect caecotroph production and this then leads to repercussions on the digestive process.

Remember, ***any gastro-intestinal stasis requires immediate treatment*** to stimulate gut motility as soon as possible. This is not a condition which can be left until tomorrow. We cannot over-emphasise the importance of prompt action in this illness and an urgent visit to a rabbit-savvy vet is strongly advised for a professional diagnosis and advice. Don't be fobbed off with the response I once received from a vet clearly with no understanding of a rabbit with gastric stasis: *"bring her back in 2-3 days if she's still not eaten or drunk anything, and we'll open her up..."*. You <u>can</u> help and it is important that you do so or your rabbit might die.

'Fur-balls'

- (trichobezoars) are caused by your rabbit swallowing too much surplus fur in the normal course of self-grooming. They are most common in longer-haired breeds (Angora and Cashmere) and during periods of moult.

In the stomach, this ingested fur combines with eaten food and can form a large mass which can block the stomach exit or caecum. As a result, the stomach remains full although no food or nutrients are passing through and the rabbit is slowly starving to death. With the large, blocked stomach or caecum, the rabbit will feel full and stop eating and drinking. Soon he will begin to bloat and swell. This process can happen very quickly, particularly in warm weather when dehydration can be rapid and should be treated as a veterinary emergency.

Normally, furballs are largely prevented by:
- regular grooming to remove excess fur and
- feeding a high fibre diet to keep fur passing through.

In-between moults your rabbit should be groomed at least twice every week. During moults, your rabbit may need to be groomed twice-daily for 2-3 weeks. However, some rabbits seem to experience a more rapid moult where they shed their coat in just a few days. In these cases, you can't afford to neglect or skip any grooming sessions. Their fur tends to fall out in clumps and is so easily ingested. Much surplus fluff can be plucked out with your fingers but an additional run-through with a shedding comb over the entire body is strongly advised because these remove loose fur very efficiently.

Eating a high fibre diet with lots of hay helps the fur to pass through the stomach and intestines to be expelled in the droppings. However, if the rabbit isn't eating enough fibre then fur can clump together in the stomach. Early signs of excessive ingestion can be seen when your rabbit passes droppings which are strung together with fur, often referred to as a 'string of pearls' and are normally about 4-8cm long.

In one memorable case, our Dwarf Lop, Maddie, had been off-colour for two weeks, with lack of appetite but despite x-rays and a full array of blood tests, her specialist vet could find no reason for her anorexia and she seemed in perfect health. The reason became clear when she produced this unprecedented 70cm long string of poo. Needless to say, once she'd passed this, she made an overnight recovery and tucked into a hearty breakfast the following morning.

All rabbits should ideally eat a loose pile of hay or grass equivalent to their body size every day and it is essential to pluck or comb away any loose fur to prevent it being ingested.

The rabbit will refuse to eat and gradually waste away. Gentle palpation of the stomach and/or X-ray can locate the furball which is usually in or around the caecum area.

One sometimes-helpful remedy is to administer 10ml of raw pineapple juice (not tinned or pineapple squash!) which contains the enzyme bromelain, or papaya which can help to break down the furball.

However, this can only be considered an amateur treatment and veterinary treatment must be sought. Offering fresh veg can also help keep a gut moist to help prevent gut contents becoming dry, harder to pass and more likely to cause a blockage.

Malt pastes

Malt pastes, available for cats, can be beneficial in helping ingested fur to pass through rabbits and can be used as a preventative treatment during periods of heavy moult and when excess fur is evident in droppings or 'strings of pearls' are produced. These pastes are usually enjoyed by rabbits and 1cm of paste may be eagerly licked off your finger. If not, add 1cm of paste to your rabbit's front paws and s/he will almost certainly groom instantly and lick it off making for very easy administration. During a heavy moult, we would administer paste up to four times daily, guided largely by the appearance of droppings in the litter tray.

Ample quantities of hay must also be given during treatment and recovery.

Simple remedies available for digestive problems

Probiotics

A probiotic such as AviPro or Protexin, is highly recommended for all cases of digestive upset. This can help restore gut bacteria and its pleasant taste encourages rabbits to drink which helps prevent dehydration.

Oral rehydration

We recommend the use of Lectade powder which is mixed with water to provide an oral rehydration solution containing vitamins, minerals and electrolytes. In an emergency, a simple solution can be made at home using one litre of cooled boiled water to which half a teaspoon of sea salt, a teaspoon of baking soda (not baking powder) and two teaspoons of sugar should be added.

Protexin Fibreplex

is a carrot-flavour paste containing 34% dietary fibre in a graduated syringe for easy administration. It is available in 15ml syringes with a recommended dosage of 1ml per kg of body weight three times daily.

Protexin Pro-Kolin+

is a kaolin and prebiotic paste suitable to treating mild cases of diarrhoea. The packaging doesn't specify a dosage but we give approximately 1ml per 2.5kg body weight, three times daily using the 30ml syringe pack (the 60ml is offers better value but is quite unwieldy for use with rabbits). Despite its beef flavour, rabbits seem to love it!

Science Recovery Plus

is a high-fibre nutritionally-complete liquid feed which can be syringe-fed to rabbits and other small furries. It can help sustain the patient during recovery and help to keep a gut moving until they resume eating normally again.

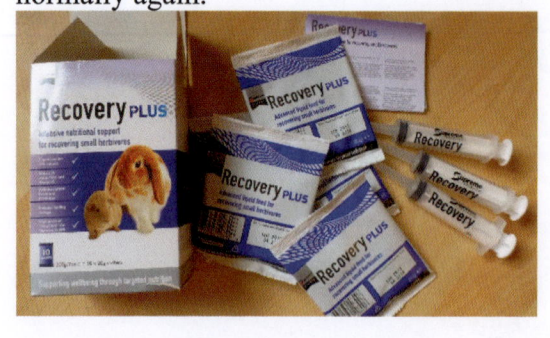

Syringe-feeding

Whenever your rabbit is ill, the chances are that he/still will suffer from a loss of appetite and refuse to eat and drink.

Due to the anatomical peculiarities of rabbits, it is absolutely **essential** that their stomachs never become empty since this results in sluggish gut motility or even a possible 'shut-down' of the GI tract. When this happens, the intestines fill with mucus, motility is lost and the rabbit feels 'full' then begins to swell and bloat, i.e. gastric stasis.

To help prevent such conditions taking hold, your rabbit must be syringe-fed. One of the best solutions to use is Supreme 'Recovery Plus' solution – a fine powder which is mixed with warm water to produce a nutritious, fibre-rich solution which is easily syringe-fed and rabbits enjoy it. Alternatively, you could crush their usual pellets, mix with warm water and syringe these instead. Pellets such as Excel and Science Selective are especially good for crushing and we always keep a bag on hand specifically for this purpose. Grind the pellets to a dust using a rolling pin then add warmed water to make a mushy paste to which you can add a little probiotic or supplement feed such as Oxbow Critical Care powder then syringe it slowly into your rabbit.

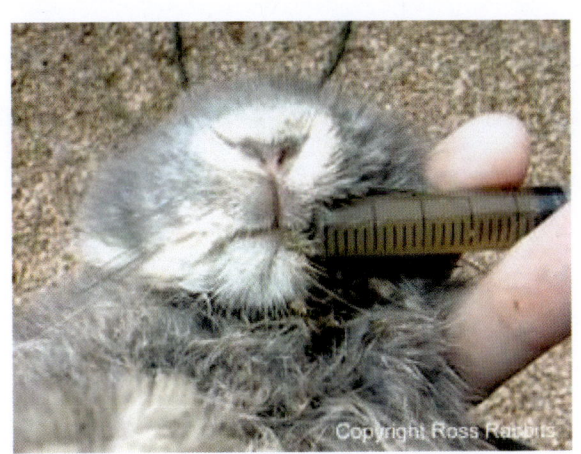

Syringe-feeding

To syringe-feed, insert the tip of the syringe behind the front teeth as shown in the photograph, point it to the **side** of your rabbit's mouth and release about 0.25- 0.5ml at a time. Wait for him/her to swallow and take **two** breaths to ensure a relaxed pace, then release another 0.25-0.5ml depending on the size of your rabbit. Some rabbits will only swallow when their mouth is full while others will greedily lap up syringe contents, so let them dictate the pace of feeding. It can be a slow process but rushing it risks choking or aspirating it into the lungs.

Never aim the syringe at the back of the throat as this may cause your rabbit to aspirate the fluid which leads to a rapid death in your hands. If you see any of the syringed fluid coming out of the nostrils, this is a warning sign that the fluid is entering the respiratory tract rather than heading down the oesophagus. So, please adapt your technique instantly. Some vegetarian, sugar-free, baby foods are also suitable for syringe feeding. If you don't feel confident, a vet nurse at your local surgery will be able to show you how to do this. If your rabbit becomes messy then he might need to be wiped clean or bathed.

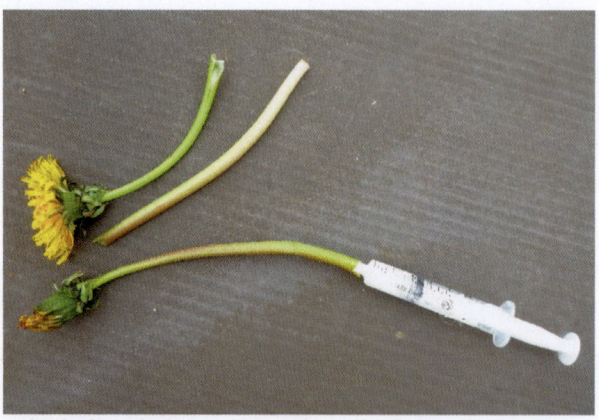

One of our methods for administering oral medications – inside the stem of a juicy dandelion

If you are unable to syringe-feed adequate fluids, then it is safest to take your rabbit to a veterinary surgeon for intravenous or subcutaneous fluids which are more effective. In an emergency, a simple oral rehydration solution can be made at home using one litre of cooled boiled water to which half a teaspoon of sea salt, a teaspoon of baking soda (not baking powder) and two teaspoons of sugar should be added.

Protexin Fibreplex is a carrot-flavour paste containing 34% dietary fibre in a graduated syringe for easy administration, is a good supplement when syringe-feeding and for emergency use. It is available in 15ml syringes with a recommended dosage of 1ml per kg of body weight three times daily.

Syringe-feeding a very co-operative rabbit

Sticky Bottom

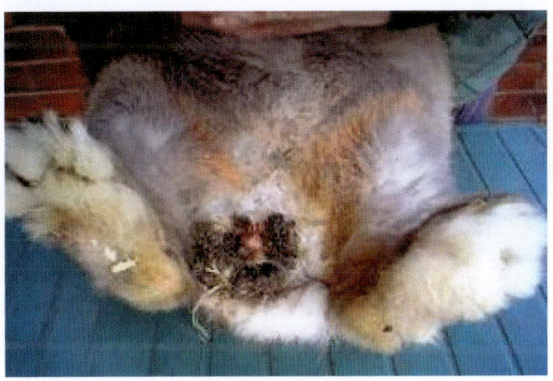

A messy bum!

'Sticky Bottom' is the graphic description of a rabbit who has a brown sticky mess around his rear end – but not diarrhoea. Unless removed, after a few days this will harden and your rabbit could soon be lugging around a heavy clump of stale, solid droppings and caecotrophs which, by this time, might need to be carefully cut away with scissors. Please ensure your rabbit's bottom never becomes caked in filth in this manner.

Normally rabbits should eat their caecotroph pellets direct from their anus. However, if they don't and choose to sit on them instead, they soon squash and become matted in your rabbit's fur which, apart from looking and smelling unpleasant, can attract flies.

If your rabbit is producing excessive caecotrophs, this could indicate:

Dietary Excess: Your rabbit might be receiving too much protein and/or carbohydrate in his/her diet, or inadequate hay and chooses to eat pellets or mix rather than caecotrophs. This is easily remedied by reducing the mix or pellets offered and increasing hay, grass and forage in the diet. This more closely resembles the diet your rabbit would have in the wild. Aim for your rabbit to eat a loose pile of meadow hay equal to his/her body size each day.

Tooth or Mouth Problems: Your rabbit might have teeth problems and a painful mouth. If this is the case then s/he won't be grooming well either and this could be an indication of a potential problem which can be investigated by your vet. Drooling around the chin can indicate molar spurs while any malocclusion of the incisors will be visibly apparent when gently pushing back the lips to look at the front teeth.

Physical problems: Your rabbit could be overweight and unable to actually reach their anus. This is seen mostly in large, overweight rabbits, particularly females with a well-developed dewlap. Also, elderly or arthritic rabbits might have difficulty bending. If your rabbit is overweight and needs to slim down, a short-term diet of grass, meadow hay, veg and water will do no harm for a few weeks.

Eye disorders

Cataracts

A cataract is an opaque film on the lens of the eye with either part of the eye being clouded or fully clouded. These can be present from birth, develop due to infection such as E. Cuniculi or appear without obvious cause.

When a cataract develops seemingly spontaneously in adulthood, it can be alarming for the rabbit who will have cloudy vision from the eye, if any vision at all. The rabbit is likely to appear distressed, disorientated, nervous and possibly unsteady although after a few days, they seem to adapt well to single-eyed vision then continue to live a normal life.

A vet should be consulted at the first sign of any eye disorder to diagnose any underlying cause and treat any infection. Surgery is possible which will involve removing the eye then neatly stitching the wound which soon heals, fur re-grows and the rabbit looks almost normal and as though the missing eye is just closed.

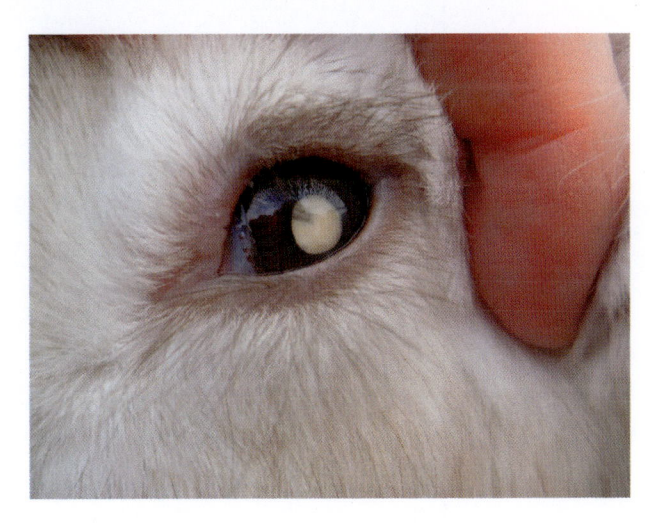

Chronic Conjunctivitis

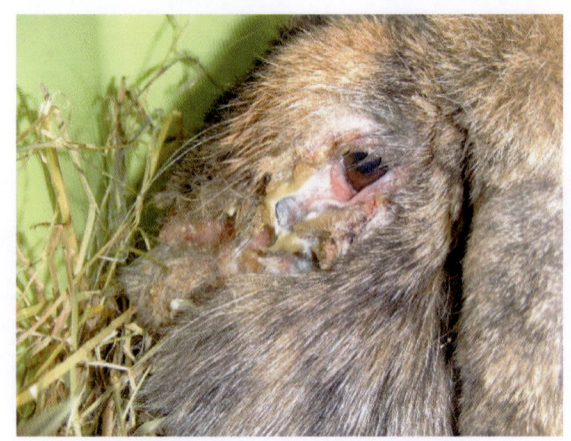

A sticky eye with milky discharge

Rabbits have a third eyelid which can occasionally be seen partially covering the eye or, more usually, towards the front corner of the eye.

Clear image of third eyelid on British Giant rabbit

Runny eyes, sometimes with a white discharge, can be caused by

• Infection such as Pasteurella multocida, Bordetella, or Staphylococcus
• An abnormality of the eyelids e.g. entropion whereby the lids turn inwards and rub the eye which can result in painful eye ulcers. Surgery is usually required to correct the abnormality.

- Blocked tear ducts which can be simply flushed by your vet
- Irritation e.g. by fine particles of sawdust or hay which can cause local irritation (easily resolved by removing irritants from the hutch)
- A high concentration of ammonia especially in male rabbits' hutches

In cases of infection, the eyelids will appear swollen and the conjunctiva will be red. The discharge from the eye can cause a loss of fur from the medial corner of the eye downwards.

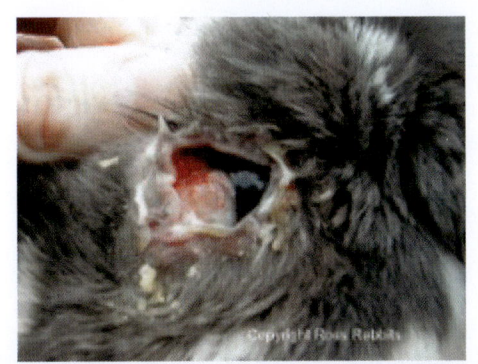

Sticky eyes in French Lop and inflammation of third eyelid

If your rabbit's tear ducts are blocked then these will need to be flushed through which is a very simple procedure carried out by your vet. However, in many persistent cases of runny eyes, no blockages are found and some research is suggesting that the problem of runny eyes might actually be caused by the rabbit suffering from **dry eyes**. The dryness of the eye could cause some irritation leading to redness and watering. This can be tested for using tear testing strips inserted into the eyelid for 1 minute. This problem appears to be most common in French Lops.

Conjunctivitis can be treated by:
- Administering antibiotic eye drops if Pasteurella or other infection is suspected
- Regular hutch-cleaning to control ammonia
- Using alternative bedding and litter

When administering prescribed ear drops, stand your rabbit on a stable surface, raise the upper eyelid and turn it back slightly then squeeze the prescribed number of drops under the lid. Your rabbit probably won't enjoy this experience very much and will try to pull away. When he closes his eye, the drops will then be applied direct to the conjunctive and any surplus will run into the lower lid.

If the discharge is not infection-related then the best way to remove excess moisture from the area is to let your rabbit's hutch-mate lick his/her eyes for him/her. Your rabbit will probably sit perfectly still and relaxed while having his eyes licked – and rabbits do seem to enjoy this very much. It's also highly effective!

Other treatments, depending on the cause, could include bathing with warm, used tea bags or colloidal silver.

Eye Ulcers

Another fairly common eye problem is eye ulcers. These can either be caused by infection or injury such as a scratch to the surface of the eye.

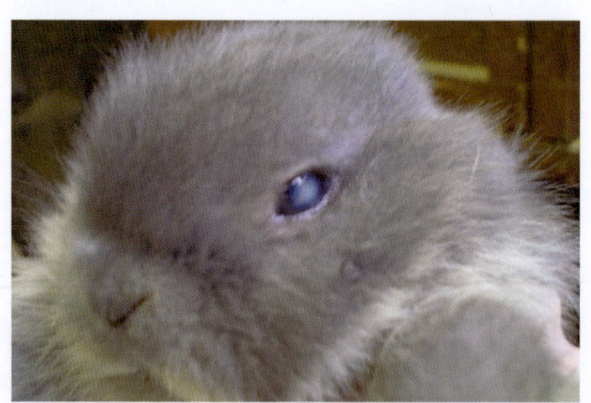

Eye ulcer on young Netherland Dwarf

Some babies are seemingly born with them so when they open their eyes at about 18 days of age, pus oozes out and an eye ulcer is exposed on the surface of the eye. If this is treated promptly and regularly bathed, ulcers can heal within 3-4 weeks but we have known a few rabbits have lifelong problems with them.

Veterinary advice must always be sought to determine and treat the cause and an antibiotic such as gentamycin will probably be required.

Eye ulcer and entropion on French Lop

Neurological Disorders

E. Cuniculi

A French Lop with splayed front legs
(for illustrative purposes only)

Encephalitozoon Cuniculi (E. Cuniculi) is a fairly common condition in pet rabbits but usually remains latent. However, it is a condition which began to attract increasing veterinary interest from 2002-3 and there is increasing research assessing its prevalence in the pet-rabbit population and the frequency of symptoms it may cause. Some vets believe it is a major health issue while others feel it is relatively harmless. It has also been guessimated that a third of pet rabbits may be asymptomatic carriers.

E. Cuniculi is caused by a parasite transmitted via spores in rabbit urine hence is easily spread from an infected mother to her young litter or rabbits coming into contact with each other's urine. It can also be spread via other species and can survive in the environment for a month so all rabbits running outdoors, or sharing a litter tray or within urine-spraying distance can be at risk.

After ingesting the parasites from an infected rabbit's urine, they move via the bloodstream to the kidneys and other organs. Within the kidney, they replicate and are shed via the urine and the rabbit is considered contagious. Next, the parasite passes through the blood-brain barrier and can affect brain cells leading to neurological damage. It affects the central nervous system by causing microscopic lesions which will only be identified at autopsy. However, many rabbits will not develop symptoms of disease.

The only way to be certain whether a rabbit is carrying E. Cuniculi is to have a blood sample analysed for antibodies to E. Cuniculi. However, this can only indicate that the rabbit has been exposed to E. Cuniculi and an immune response has occurred. The greater the infection and the more recent exposure has been then the higher the antibody titre reading will be. But this does not confirm, or otherwise, that the rabbit will develop symptoms.

If they do show symptoms, these can include:-
- Paralysis
- Splay leg: the rabbit flops with legs (usually hind legs) splayed out to each side
- Cloudy eyes/cataracts – particularly in young rabbits
- Torticollis (head rolling/head tilt)
- Seizures

Other indications can include the following (but can also be caused by other conditions such as diabetes):
- Excessive drinking
- Urine scald (normal grooming can then produce re-exposure to the spores expelled in the urine)
- Weight loss

There is no known effective treatment although wormers such as Valbazen/Albendazole and Panacur/Fenbendazole have been anecdotally noted to reduce the titre count in blood serum samples and control or reduce symptoms either initially or in future relapses.

If E. Cuniculi is confirmed via a blood test, then it is probable that the rabbit will be treated with Panacur for a month and this will be followed by a further blood test. Treatment may then be continued and followed by further blood tests.

Some infected rabbits with symptoms will live for years, enjoying a normal happy, healthy and active life without showing any signs of illness, even with a high titre level.

EC alone does not necessarily even affect the rabbit's general health so a high titre level is not a sign of terminal illness. However, if the rabbit is already suffering from other illnesses putting their immune system under strain, the risks to the rabbit are then increased. EC alone is seldom a cause of death although it can be a contributing factor in a rabbit who is already ill or has a compromised immune system.

If a rabbit should be unlucky enough to develop neurological symptoms or disability, then s/he will usually adapt and continue to live a relatively normal life in-between flare-ups.

Epilepsy

Epilepsy can occur in breeds with white fur and blue eyes such as the Beveren White, Vienna White and Belgian breeds although it is not a common illness.

If your rabbit appears to be experiencing seizures, then they might be caused by epilepsy but seizures are also linked with other causes, such as:-

- E. Cuniculi – a parasite which affects the brain cells (symptoms also include torticollis (i.e. head rolling), hind limb paralysis and incontinence)
- Arteriosclerosis of blood vessels in the brain
- Abscesses in the brain
- Brain tumours
- VHD – immediately prior to death
- Liver disease
- Fly strike (Myasis)

Death can occur during a seizure.

Note re fits: It is also common for a rabbit to appear to have a 'fit' immediately prior to death and the kicking of limbs can continue, as a reflex action, for a few minutes following death which can be alarming for unprepared owners to witness.

Floppy Bunny Syndrome

Floppy Bunny Syndrome refers to an otherwise seemingly health rabbit suddenly found completely floppy, usually on their abdomen rather than their side, with absolutely no muscle tone and sometimes splayed front legs. On picking them up or trying to rearrange their limbs, they are completely limp and floppy with limbs hanging. Body temperature is usually normal, hydration good, eyes clear and bright and there are no obvious signs of illness.

The cause is poorly understood with anecdotal tales of vitamin or potassium deficiency or possible poisoning but nothing conclusive.

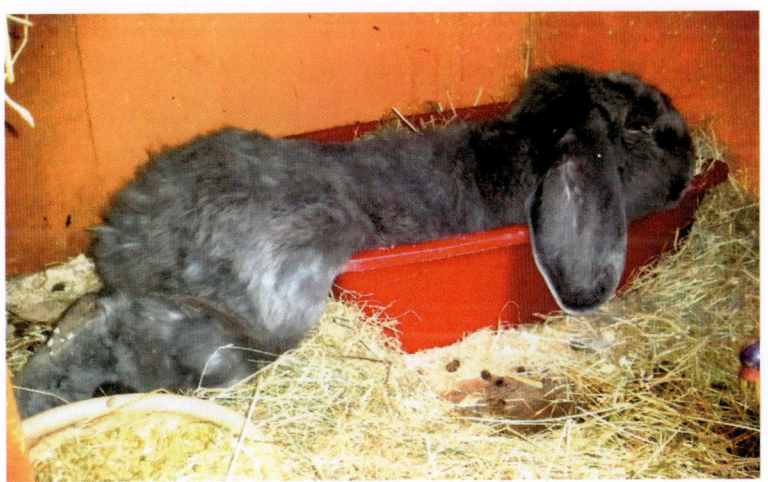

French Lop found with floppy bunny syndrome
A week later she had made a full recovery.

Despite having no muscle tone and being unable to move, affected rabbits in our experience, can and do eat. We've had about 3 cases in over 40 years and all have survived. We cover place the affected rabbit on a soft bed of barley straw with absorbent litter beneath, cover the body lightly in hay for warmth and insulation then place handfuls of wet grass, wet dandelion leaves, slices of banana, small pieces of apple or carrot slices and other favourite forage in front of the mouth. The rabbit usually tucks in hungrily and we replace through the day and night. As the rabbit recovers we then place a small low bowl or saucer of water so the rabbit can drink and continue providing favourite foods, mostly wet where possible to ensure the rabbit remains well hydrated for minimal effort and continue replenishing hay over the body as this is eaten.

Recovery usually takes about 4-8 days and our rabbits have always made a full recovery and continued to live full and active lives with no relapse.

Head Tilt (Torticollis)

Torticollis refers to the 'rolling' movements of the head which can be caused by infection of the middle ear which can be due to Pasteurella or E. Cuniculi or other vestibular causes.

It can be very distressing and disorienting for the poor rabbit who could be viewing his world from a very strange angle and probably feeling rather 'seasick'. Indirectly, this can affect appetite or the rabbit might actually be unable to eat and drink and will need to be syringe-fed.

It can improve with a long-term course of antibiotics. Affected rabbits also seem to appreciate a gentle neck massage, particularly on the affected side.

The above photograph shows a slight head tilt in a French Lop recovering from torticollis. At its worst, her head was completely 'tipped over' and she was very unbalanced and wobbly when walking. Picking her up caused some distress as her body wanted to twist one way while her head went the other way.

Although an outdoor rabbit, she was brought indoors for treatment and confined to a small indoor cage to help keep her propped up and minimise any movement which caused her distress. If we removed her, such as for cleaning, on popping her back into her recovery cage, she was very disorientated and would fall onto her side taking a while to adjust and sit up again.

This Netherland Dwarf looks relatively 'normal' or even 'cute' but she has a bad case. Like the above French Lop, any attempts to pick her up would make her extremely uncomfortable and upset her balance so that she would roll onto her back, twist and be unable to right herself again. Hence, she was propped up against a hutch wall and received antibiotic injections without being moved. She managed to eat and drink easily and even maintained her own personal hygiene.

Recovery is notoriously slow. The French Lop made a full recovery but the torticollis returned a few months later.

If thought to be related to E. Cuniculi then a precautionary course of Fenbendazole or Albendazole can be given while oxytetracycline and/or prochlorperazine may be prescribed for vestibular symptoms.

Paralysis

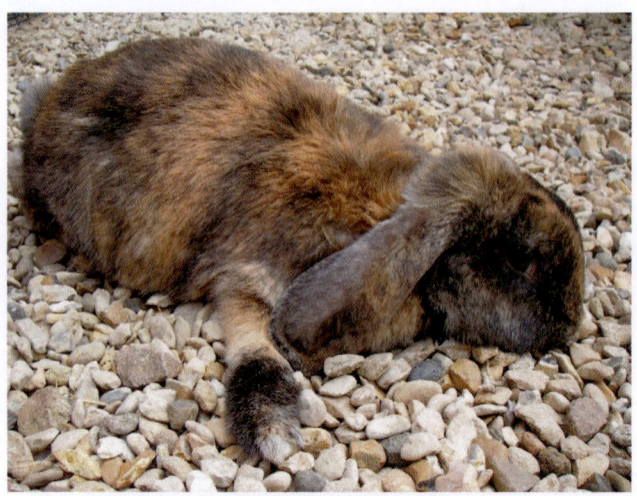

Paralysed rabbit with splayed front legs

Paralysis can be temporary or permanent and can have a number of causes:

Encephalitozoon Cuniculi (E. C.) is caused by the E. Cuniculi parasite, is a frequent cause of paralysis and the rabbit may also display a wry neck (torticollis) and rolling movements. There is no 100% effective treatment known at present although some wormers, such as Panacur (Fenbendazole), can help reduce the blood titre level.

Coccidiosis - paralysis of the hind legs can occur in severe cases. The rabbit can regain its mobility.

Injury: fractured or dislocated lumbar vertebrae - a rabbit's spine is not very flexible and can be damaged by poor handling, particularly dropping from a height. In the case of a broken back the prognosis is poor and the paralysis, along with incontinence, will be permanent. If the paralysis is caused by dislocation of the vertebrae rather than a break, recovery is possible. An x-ray can detect a fracture, dislocation or inflammation of the spinal cord.

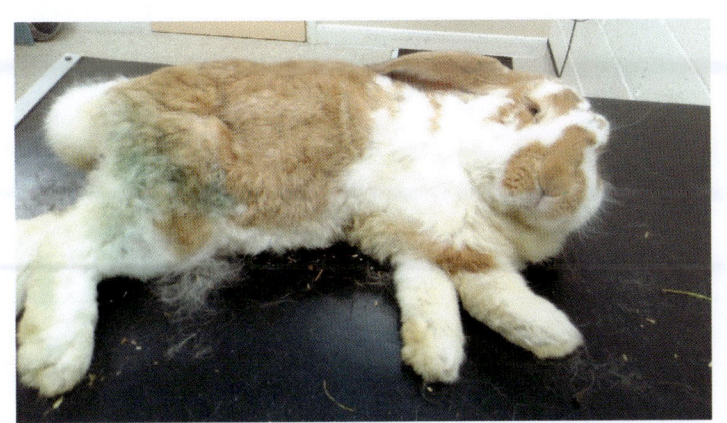

Paralysed rabbit, Wally, with T9-10 spinal fracture.
He could raise his head but was otherwise paralysed.

Fly strike (Myasis)

Fly Strike is a very serious illness which can rapidly lead to death in an otherwise healthy rabbit.

Flies are attracted to rabbits whose coats are soiled with urine, faeces or sticky caecotrophs, particularly around their anus where the skin can be warm and moist providing a perfect breeding ground for maggots. If your rabbit's coat should ever become heavily soiled with urine, diarrhoea or caecotrophs, then she/he will need to be bathed.

Flies will lay their eggs on warm, moist, soiled skin or open wounds and within 24 hours the affected rabbit can be stricken with a severe maggot infestation leading to a terminal state of shock. They will eat away at external tissue, particularly open wounds or the vulva in females and then start to eat their way into the rabbit, usually in the genital region. Often, the first signs of this will be seen when you tip your rabbit onto his/her back and see the genital area swarming with maggots.

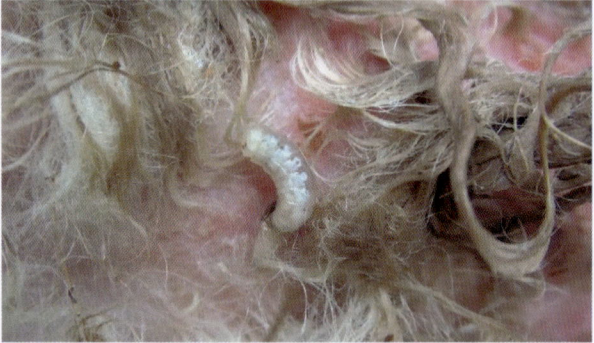

Single maggot

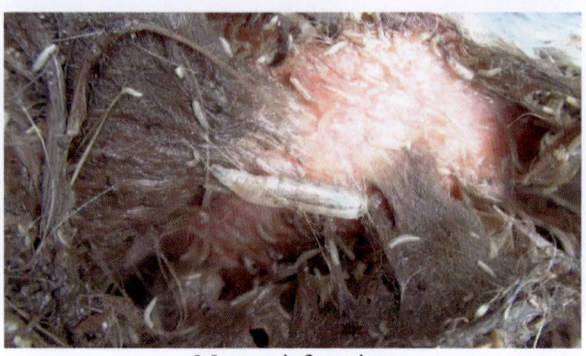

Maggot infestation

It only takes one single fly to lay eggs in a warm spot and, once they've hatched, the maggots will eat away external skin and debris and then move internally inside the flesh where they produce toxins which create a state of shock. Internal maggots cannot be seen but if you spot maggots around your rabbit's rear end then it is almost certain there will be some internally. Signs of infection or shock can include listlessness or even seizures.

Treatment is **urgent** and maggot infestation must be treated as an emergency. Maggots are attracted by heat so using a hair dryer on the low setting can help draw out maggots to the skin surface. Then external maggots can be carefully removed with tweezers but it is probable that there will still be some internally so an urgent visit to the vet is called for without delay. Your vet may then wash your rabbit with an insecticide solution, administer Ivermectin (or similar treatment) and antibiotics. If caught in the early stages, then the prognosis is good, but prevention is always better than cure.

The best means of preventing fly strike is to check your rabbit's rear end every morning and night to ensure it is always clean and dry. Keep hutch bedding and litter as dry as possible via regular cleaning and try to eradicate any flies buzzing around the hutch or cage, although this is easier said than done, especially for rabbits living outdoors in an open garden in hot weather.

Aerosol/chemical fly killers could potentially be harmful to rabbits so try using sticky fly papers. They look unsightly but with careful positioning, they can help a little. Alternatively, fly 'zappers' with a UV tube can be very effective in an enclosed area such as a shed but an outdoor power supply will be required unless you are able to source a less-effective battery-operated model.

Other products can help prevent flies taking interest in your rabbit's posterior, including:-

- Beaphar Fly Free
- Beaphar Fly Guard
- Rear Guard

Fly Guard and Rear Guard *(other products are available)* offers up to 10-12 weeks protection against fly strike when applied to your rabbit's vulnerable rear end prior to any anticipated attack. Although it won't repel flies, it does prevent any maggots forming and hence a blowfly attack. It can only be used on rabbits aged over 10 weeks, is not to be used by breeding does and is not a substitute for impeccable hygiene.

If your rabbit seems especially prone to a dirty bottom then this could indicate other health problems such as diarrhoea, dental problem, mobility problems or obesity preventing your rabbit keeping cleaning, incontinence or excess caecotrophs due to a diet too rich in protein. Increasing the amount of fibre in the diet can help.

Heat Stroke

Heat stroke can rapidly claim lives of rabbits in hot weather i.e. above 25°C so it is vital that you are vigilant in warm and hot weather conditions.

Prevention is easier than cure and can be achieved by keeping a hutch in a cool, shaded area of the garden or moving an indoor cage into the coolest room in the house. Free-range house-rabbits might need to be confined to a few cool rooms since your rabbit won't necessarily get up and move him/herself. Electric fans, although simply wafting hot air around, do help provide a cooling breeze although, because rabbits do not sweat like humans do, fans don't have the same benefits although rabbits do seem to like them. If you use a mains-powered fan, ensure you keep their cables well out of reach of a nibbler-rabbit. Alternatively, a USB rechargeable fan can be a safer solution or use a hair dryer on its cool setting if a fan isn't available.

Frozen bottles of water or ice packs wrapped in a thin towel or an Ice Pod, specifically designed for this purpose, will also help.

If you should find your rabbit collapsed, panting heavily with a very wet nose and mouth area, this can indicate heat stroke and you need to act fast to reduce his/her temperature before the condition rapidly becomes fatal.

If you have access to an air conditioner, then placing an over-heated rabbit in an air conditioned room can help with cooling him down.

Above: Giles has just collapsed so is quickly rushed to the coolest place in the house

The ears will feel extremely hot so try cooling these first.

Having moved your rabbit into a cool area, spraying both ears with tepid water (not cold – this can cause shock) is the quickest and easiest way to do this while you prepare some damp towels to drape your rabbit in, particularly around the head and ears. Pieces of kitchen roll soaked in cool (not cold) water are also effective.

Sit with your rabbit while s/he cools down and replace the towels/kitchen roll as soon as this dries or becomes warm. It could take a few hours before your rabbit gets up and shakes the towels off showing that he is now feeling much better.

Providing you identify the condition and act promptly, your rabbit stands a good chance of recovery. Without attention, heat stoke can kill in just 15 minutes of exposure to extreme hot temperatures.

If your rabbit has also become dehydrated, then fluid therapy will be required. In view of the urgency, this is best administered by a veterinary surgeon where possible, but not if this involves a long drive in a hot car. If a vet visit is impractical then, once the temperature has reduced, you may find your rabbit will lap up water offered from a bowl (in preference to a bottle).

Infections

Pasteurella Multocida

Pasteurella is one of the most common infections afflicting pet rabbits and pasteurellosis can cause the following respiratory symptoms:

- **'snuffles'** - sneezing, coughing, purulent nasal discharge, chronic sinusitis
- **chronic pasteurellosis** - peritonitis, metritis, mastitis, otitis media, abscess formation (internal and/or external)
- **pneumonia** with breathing difficulties

It is a common infection and many, apparently healthy rabbits will carry the bacteria but display no symptoms of infection. However, a rabbit with an impaired immune system can develop a chronic form of infection.

In many cases, the rabbit will continue to carry on with his daily life, eating and drinking normally, but wiping his nose on his paw after sneezing and this matted fur can be one of the first indications of the disease. As a general rule of paw, if nasal discharge is white, green or yellow, then this can indicate infection. A clear discharge is more likely to be an allergy, but it's always advisable to check with your vet.

Veterinary attention is required together with a course of antibiotic treatment. Fluoroquinolone antibiotic Enrofloxacin (Baytril), by mouth, or injected oxytetracyclines are the drugs of choice although their effectiveness can be limited to controlling rather than completely eliminating the infection.

Secondary infections can prove fatal.

Pneumonia

Mouth-breathing rabbit with advanced pneumonia

If your rabbit is holding his head high and/or has laboured, snuffly breathing with possible crackly sounds heard from the lungs, this can indicate advanced pneumonia. The kindest option might be immediate euthanasia to prevent further suffering, particularly if your rabbit also has blue gum tissues indication low oxygen.

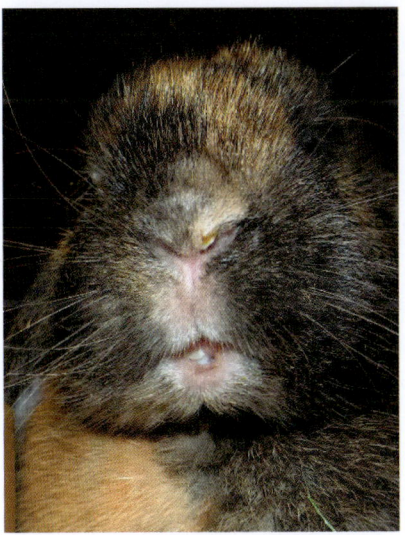

Mouth-breathing rabbit with advanced pneumonia

Skin and fur problems

Rabbits can be prone to a number of skin problems – most of which can be treated very simply.

The most common problems include:

- Moulting
- Simple Cuts
- Sore Hocks (sores on the feet)
- Infestations: Mites and fleas

Moulting

Rabbits usually have two major moults per year in the early and late summer.

In the early stages of the moult, there can be some skin irritation as the old fur falls out and is slowly replaced by the new, thicker, glossier coat. Moulting starts around the forehead and shoulders then extends across the back with the lower sides and underside being the last to shed. Often there is a 'tide mark' line of tinged fur between the new glossy coat and the older, ragged, shedding coat. Sometimes the moult is slow around the flanks and just above the tail – areas which are less accessible for your rabbit to reach. In these areas, we strongly advise offering your rabbit some help and combing out or plucking out the old fur which is likely to become clumpy or matted around here.

During this time, it is very important that you groom your rabbit regularly using a shedding comb to remove loose fur and prevent excessive amounts being ingested which can lead to sluggish gastric motility and furballs.

Tip: If you have a rabbit prone to sore hocks then it is worth saving some of the fluff . This can be used to make padded cushions to fit inside bandages. Natural bunny fluff is much better than any synthetic padding!

Furballs occur when too much surplus loose fur is swallowed by your rabbit as he grooms himself. In the stomach, this combines with food and can, in the early stages, produces a string of joined-together droppings which can be an early sign that excess fur is being ingested. When this happens, feed extra hay and groom your rabbit at least twice-daily to remove excess fur and administer a malt paste used to prevent/treat fur-balls in cats. If too much excess fur is swallowed this can form a huge mass which then blocks the stomach exit. As a result, the rabbit's stomach remains full and feels large although no nutrients are passing through and your rabbit is slowly starving. With the large stomach, your rabbit will feel full and stop eating and drinking and will soon begin to bloat and swell. This process can happen very quickly, particularly in warm weather when dehydration can be rapid and should be treated as a veterinary emergency. However, the condition can be largely prevented by regular grooming sessions.

Malt pastes, available for cats, can be beneficial in helping ingested fur to pass through rabbits. It can be used as a preventative during periods of heavy moult and when excess fur is evident in droppings or 'strings of pearls' are produced. The pastes are usually enjoyed by rabbits and 1cm of paste may be eagerly licked off your finger. If not, add 1cm of paste to your rabbit's front paws and s/he will almost certainly groom instantly and lick it off making for very easy administration. During a heavy moult, we would administer paste up to four times daily, guided largely by the appearance of droppings in the litter tray.

Simple cuts

Like humans, rabbits can be prone to the occasional cut or scratch. In these cases, simply trim the fur surrounding the cut or scratch, bathe the wound and apply a pet-safe antiseptic ointment. Aloe Vera-based products can be good for rabbits. There is a strong possibility your rabbit may try to lick it off within minutes so a long snuggle on your knee will allow time for it to be absorbed. For larger wounds, these may need vet attention for stitching.

Sore hocks (feet)

Unlike cats and dogs, rabbits do not have paw-pads so take their body weight on their large, flat hind feet which may be only sparsely furred. When housed on a flat or hard floor, the rabbit's toe nails force the feet into an unnatural angle so greater body weight is taken towards the heels. If housed on bedding of deep shavings topped with soft barley straw or even a grass lawn, the toe nails curl into this and weight is spread more evenly across the surface of the foot making sores less likely.

Foot sores are most commonly found on the larger, heavier breeds such as Giants and French Lops where the combination of heavy body weight and, sometimes, thinly-furred paws and feet, leads to the formation of painful sores. Rex breeds also tend to have only lightly-furred feet so area also prone to sores developing on their heals and hind feet. With any open wounds on feet, there is always a risk that they can ulcerate, infection enter the wound, spread up the leg and enter the bloodstream leading to a more serious systemic staphylococcus infection. Deep sores can also penetrate to the artery leading to haemorrhage.

We advise providing thick, soft, absorbent bedding such as deep, fine wood shavings topped with soft barley straw for rabbits prone to sore hocks or for rabbits undergoing treatment.

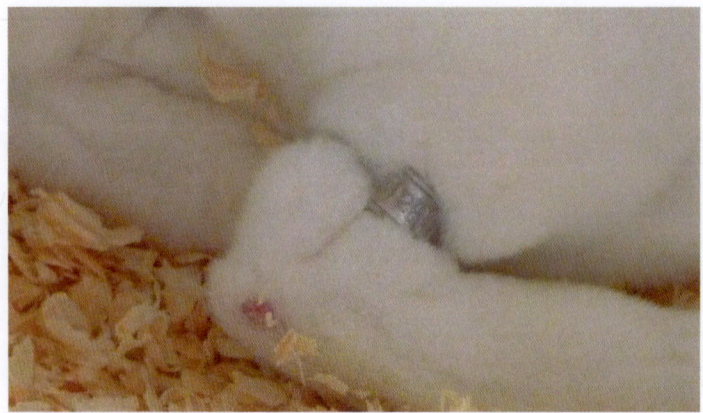

Sore foot – an over-tight leg ring and small sore on the heel

The above rabbit has a small sore on his heel but also had a leg ring fitted as a youngster which is now too tight. This was removed and then his foot was treated.

Small, non-advanced surface-sores can be home-treated. Povidone iodine is useful for disinfecting the skin and Supremo, used to treat nappy rash, is a good barrier cream. Preparation H, more commonly used to treat haemorrhoids in humans, can sometimes be helpful in treating sores on paws.

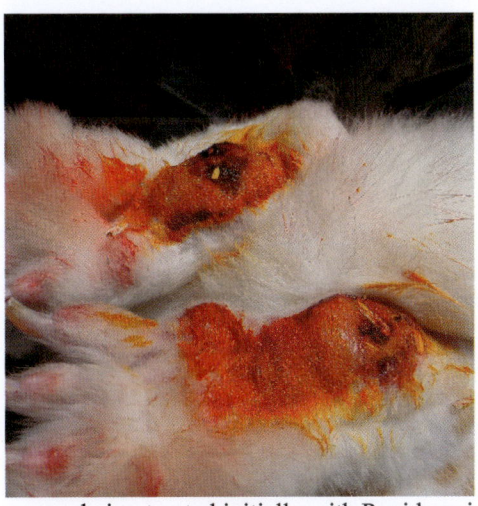

Advanced ulcerating sores being treated initially with Povidone iodine to cleanse the skin

In all but the simplest cases, veterinary advice should be sought to obtain an antibiotic ointment to apply or even systemic antibiotics if the wound has already become infected. Severe cases might need bandaging, but it can be quite a challenge to find a rabbit who will tolerate having his paws and feet in socks!

To make a bandage, use a length of 'Vet-Wrap' bandage which adheres to itself and split it into two strips at each end leaving the centre joined in an 'H' shape. A pad of fur saved from a moult can be added to help relieve pressure on the sore area. With the horizontal section of the 'H' on the heal, wrap two of the straps around the ankle and the lower two straps around the foot to make a 'boot'. To allow full foot mobility, clip a hole at the front of the ankle so that it can flex. Ensure it is not too tight or cutting into the skin or too slack causing it to fall off . Good luck - most rabbits dislike this and will do their utmost to sabotage your efforts to help them!

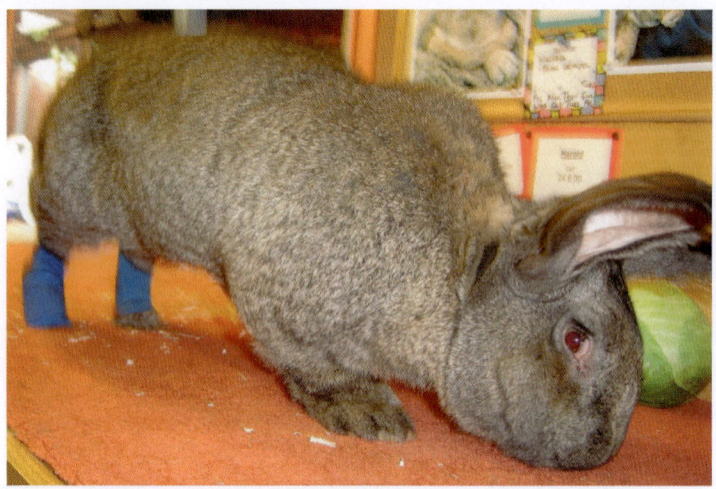

Wallace, a Continental Giant, with his foot bandages

Mites

Mites are quite common in pet rabbits and can cause itching, scaly skin and a loss of fur on the back. Moult normally just produces a loss of fur, starting at the shoulders and then extending down the back to the sides and, finally, the underside. During this time, your rabbit might look quite 'ragged' and untidy but the new coat will soon come through, thick and glossy.

A moult can also draw attention to a mite problem via the scaling skin which provides a nutrition source for these unwanted 'little visitors'.

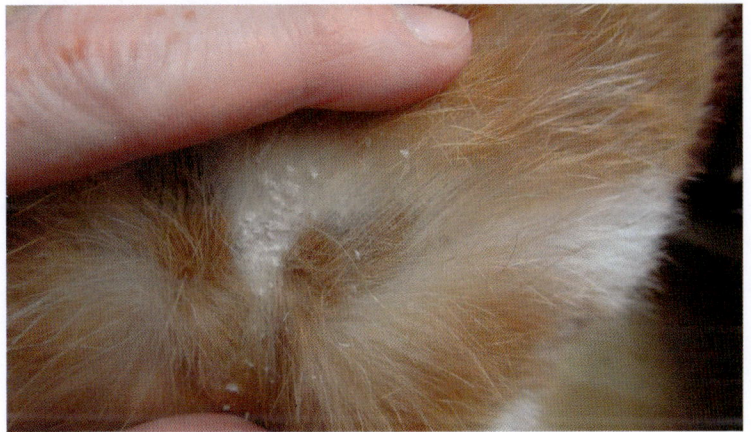

Checking for skin flaking and 'visitors'

During periods of moulting a rabbit will experience fur loss and possibly some skin irritation and it can sometimes be difficult to distinguish between a normal moult and infestation with mites so a skin scraping might be required for examination under your vet's microscope.

There are several different types of mites which can affect rabbits:
- Cheyletiella parasitosis
- Fur mites
- Dermanyssus gallinae (red fowl mite)
- Demodex Cuniculi

Cheyletiella Parasitovorax

These are small mites which cannot be seen by the naked eye and are sometimes referred to as 'mange mites'. They feed on keratin and are usually found around the nape and just above the tail, i.e. in areas which are harder to reach and groom and hence where older fur tends to accumulate.

Signs of flaking skin or dandruff on the nape or back often indicate a Cheyletiella infestation. The dandruff appears to move which is caused by the movements of the mites below. If your rabbit has any of these symptoms, then it is best to seek veterinary advice to confirm whether there is a mite infestation which can be treated very easily. Regular grooming reduces the amount of old fur in your rabbit's coat and thus reduces food sources for the mites.

Affected rabbits can feel uncomfortable and frequently scratch but the condition can pass un-noticed. However, these mites can carry myxomatosis so it is important to treat your rabbit and ensure s/he is up to date with his/her myxomatosis vaccinations. The mites can also be passed to humans so if you develop a raised, red, itchy rash…..

(Are you scratching as you read this?!)

Fur Mites

These are relatively common and it is possible to see mites with the naked eye: they appear as tiny, dark specks on a light coat which, when watched closely, move up and down fur strands.

On a white rabbit, a large infestation can be seen as tiny black dots in a light-coloured rabbit while on a dark coat, mites can appear as white specks suggesting mites are actually dual-colour!

Part the fur and look closely for the tell-tale specks of the 'little visitors'.

Dermanyssus gallinae (red fowl mite): this mite can affect rabbits housed with fowl and causes restlessness.

Demodex Cuniculi: This mite is thought to be found in the fur follicles of most rabbits and is not clinically significant.

Ear Mites

Itching and brown-grey scaly crusting within the ears and possibly sore, ulcerated skin beneath, can indicate ear mites which invade the ear canal causing much irritation to their host. If your rabbit is scratching his/her ears or if the base of the ear is sore then ear mites can be suspected. This usually clears with a course of Ivermectin prescribed by a vet.

Mite Treatment

Indications of mites include large patches of thick, scaly skin with the appearance of heavy dandruff. The mites damage fur follicles and fur can be pulled out in clumps, still with skin flakes/'dandruff' attached.

Treatment usually involves a course of Ivermectin (or other similar insecticide) under vet supervision. As the gestation period for the mites can be 10 days, treatment will normally be a minimum of 14 days to ensure the next generation of mites also succumb, usually with 3-4 Ivermectin injections over 14-20 days. If the infested rabbit comes into contact with other rabbits then it is often advisable to treat them too otherwise any mites these are carrying can hop back onto the original host!

Careful grooming is also advised to remove dead fur and dander i.e. a food source for fleas and mites. Ear mites require similar treatment but vets might also prescribe antibiotics to prevent/treat any bacterial infection plus painkillers where required.

Fleas

Fleas are less common in pet rabbits. However, pet rabbits can still be affected by dog and cat fleas, particularly where cats hunt for wild rabbits or frequent hedgerows where wild rabbits could be. Fleas are easily transmitted onto cats (and dogs) and these could bring them home and introduce them to your pet rabbit.

More importantly, these fleas could be carrying myxomatosis (or other diseases) which will then infect your pet rabbit(s). Hence, it is important to always ensure your rabbits are fully vaccinated.

A range of small animal insecticidal treatments, usually Ivermectin based, are available from pet supplies stores and can help treat a minor infestation if the instructions are followed methodically. However if you are in any doubt, it is recommended that you consult your veterinary surgeon for diagnosis, advice and prescription medication if required.

Home treatments for fleas and mites

Mild infestations of fleas, mites, mange mites and lice can be home-treated with low-dose preparations available from pet stores using products such as Beaphar's Anti-Parasite Spot-On. These packs include four pipettes of 150ug Ivermectin which will treat 750g rabbit body weight so a 3kg rabbit will use all four pipettes per treatment and a 6kg rabbit will require 2 packs per treatment. When multiple treatments are needed, it is probably more economic to take your rabbit for treatment by a veterinary surgeon.

Teeth and dental issues

Rabbits have a very small mouth opening so the only way it can be thoroughly examined, e.g. to check for dental problems on the molars, is by using an auriscope which can be pointed around the mouth. This is normally tolerated by a well-handled rabbit although they will attempt to chew it.

However, if your rabbit has painful spurs and resulting lacerations in his mouth then this could be too painful for him and sedation or a thorough examination under anaesthetic will be needed along with filing down any spurs or extracting loose or problematic teeth.

Other mouth issues and injuries can be diagnosed and dealt with while under anaesthetic including looking for stray grass seeds or small wooden splinters which can become implanted in the tongue, cheek or tooth root leading to painful swelling, infection or even abscess. Such foreign bodies can be removed and injuries treated and prevent a simple grass seed setting off a chain of potentially fatal gastric stasis.

Teeth and jaw anatomy

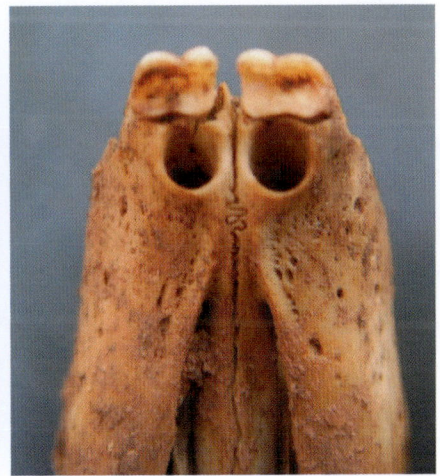

Front incisors with peg teeth immediately behind,

Like hares, rabbits are lagomorphs and have a set of 'peg' teeth immediately behind their upper incisors seen on the above skull.

Apart from the incisors, a rabbit's teeth are not easily seen.

They are arranged as:

Upper jaw, front to back: 2 front incisors in front of 2 smaller 'peg' shaped incisor, 3 premolars and 2-3 molars

Lower jaw, front to back: 2 incisors, 2 premolars, 3 molars

When viewing teeth from the front, they should appear straight with the upper incisors overlapping the lower incisors to provide the correct bite.

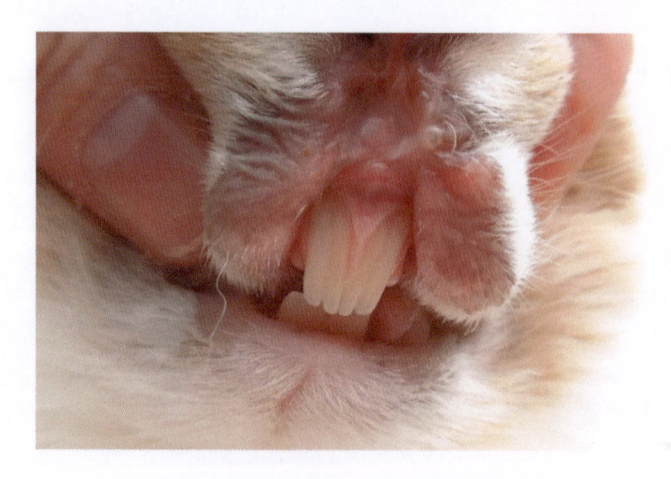

Normal, correctly aligned incisors

Above: overgrown upper incisor growing into gap left by missing lower incisor

With careful breeding, feeding the correct diet and always ensuring your rabbit has something to gnaw on, teeth problems should be only rarely experienced, if ever.

Healthy incisors should match top and bottom, with the upper incisors slightly overlapping the lower when viewed from the side, just like the human jaw and teeth.

Rabbit teeth grow continuously so if the upper and lower incisors actually meet without an overlap forming a correct bite, i.e. 'tooth to tooth', this can lead to later problems since, as they grow, they will force the jaw to remain open, causing eating difficulties.

The main problems to occur are :

Spurs

Painful overgrowths on the molar teeth which can cut into the gums and inside of the cheek causing pain when the rabbit eats. Symptoms of this can include dribbling and a reluctance to eat. Spurs can be corrected with surgery but often reoccur later. They are best prevented by feeding a diet high in hay and grass which requires lots of chewing to help keep constantly-growing teeth worn down. A rabbit who suddenly loses appetite or begins drooling should always have a dental examination to check for painful spurs developing and cutting into the tongue or inside of the cheek. Another indication of spurs can be drooling and wetness around the mouth and chin.

Note Giles is wet beneath his chin – a sign of dental issues such as molar spurs.

Malocclusion

This occurs where the upper and lower incisors are not in normal alignment.

Above: the lower incisors are growing in front of and over the upper incisors. The peg teeth can be seen behind the upper incisors.

Instead, the upper incisors can grow down into the tongue while the lower incisors grow outwards or up towards the nostrils, resembling elephants' tusks. This can make eating very difficult for the rabbit. Often the best treatment is to have them surgically removed which is a simple and permanent solution. Otherwise, very simple cases will probably need regular burring which can be stressful for both the rabbit and owner with repeated vet surgery visits and associated bills.

Incisors grow at about 2mm per week in normal alignment but in cases of malocclusion, the incisors can grow even faster to quickly become out of control as shown on this teenaged Netherland Dwarf. Some incisors will grow outward at an angle, others will grow upwards into the nostrils. It is also possible the roots will be growing too, beneath the jaw and into the lower cheek so this is not an issue which can be overlooked.

A bad case of maloccluded incisors

The best means of prevention are:

1. Careful breeding because this can be a hereditary problem, particularly with dwarf breeds due to their 'cobby' head shape.

2. Feeding the correct, highly abrasive diet to help keep teeth in trim and always ensuring your rabbit has a piece of wood, such as an apple tree branch, to gnaw on will also help to prevent teeth problems.

Tooth fracture

Occasionally a front incisor can break often as a result of a rabbit pulling on the wire bars of his cage. If incisors fracture at uneven lengths, this can force the continuously growing teeth into a tooth-to-tooth position potentially prising the jaw apart and leading to ongoing dental issues. A simple remedy is to burr the incisors into a consistent length to maintain occlusion and the rabbit should have no further problems. The burring can be undertaken without anaesthetic.

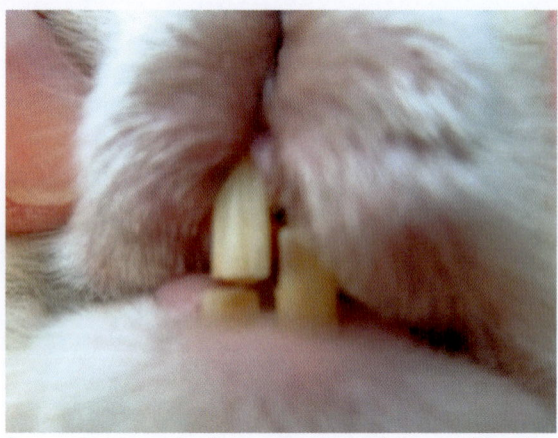

This rabbit's broken and uneven incisors were burred to matching lengths to maintain occlusion

Urinary problems

Rabbit urine can vary from deep orange, rather like fresh orange juice, to red, brown, clear or straw-coloured and is can be related to variations in the diet. None of these are a cause for concern although when owners see red urine it is often mistakenly assumed to be blood (which would only very rarely be visible) and could simply be the result of a diet of beetroot.

Rabbits excrete calcium via their urine which can make urine appear white. Occasional milky urine is normal but if it continues or becomes thick, sludgy and pasty then it can be a sign of excess calcium in the diet and difficult for the rabbit to pass without straining.

Always ensure your rabbit has access to fresh water: as a guide, a rabbit on a dry diet should drink about 50-100ml per kg body weight, possibly less in cold weather and more in hot, humid conditions.

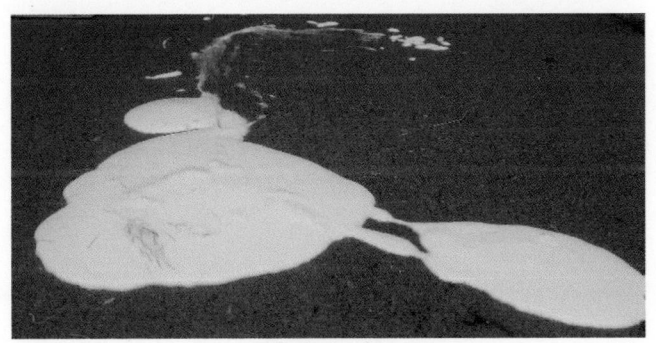

Sludgy urine

Bladder sludge

If your rabbit is sitting hunched up in pain, dribbling urine or straining to urinate then this could indicate thick, sludgy urine, a painful kidney stone or irritating bladder stone, all of which can be confirmed via X-ray.

Excess bladder sludge can be uncomfortable and may require either a vet-administered bladder-flush or encouraging the rabbit to do this him/herself by giving subcutaneous fluids together with a small dose of diazepam to relax the bladder sphincter encouraging the rabbit to void his/her bladder contents.

If your rabbit appears to be in pain while urinating or suddenly starts urinating outside the litter tray for no obvious or hormonal reasons, then this can be a symptom of cystitis which will probably require antibiotic treatment using Chloramphenicol. A confirmed diagnosis of infection can be difficult because many bladder infections are caused by anaerobic infections meaning that as soon as the bacteria come into contact with oxygen they die, hence samples obtained will always give a negative result.

In the event of any bloodstained urine, this must always be investigated to rule out any possible kidney disease, bladder stones or even uterine cancer.

Bloodstained urine – from a rabbit later diagnosed with uterine cancer
(Photo courtesy of P Halkyard)

Urine Scald

Urine scald can occur in elderly, immobile or disabled rabbits who have difficulty reaching their litter tray, the incontinent, those with EC, or due to a urinary infection such as cystitis. Rabbits with spinal injuries or other mobility issues can be unable to raise their hind-quarters and tail to urinate and direct the stream away from their body so end up soaking their coat and are unable to clean it.

Sore wet skin of urine scald

The rabbit affected is likely to feel quite sore with tender burned skin on his hind quarters, legs, feet, genital area and flanks. He will be smelly, feel heavy around the hind quarters which may affect his mobility and, due to the damp fur and skin, he is at risk of fly strike, especially in hot weather.

The cause must be addressed and treated to prevent recurrence. The rabbit will also need bathing to remove the stale urine from his coat and treat the sore damp and often raw or inflamed skin beneath.

Use warm water and a very gentle pet shampoo. After bathing and rinsing, towel dry his coat first then use a hairdryer to dry it thoroughly. Apply a soothing ointment such as Sudocrem nappy rash cream and ensure his litter tray is easily accessible and kept clean and dry. If he has limited mobility then absorbent puppy 'wee-wee' pads can be useful.

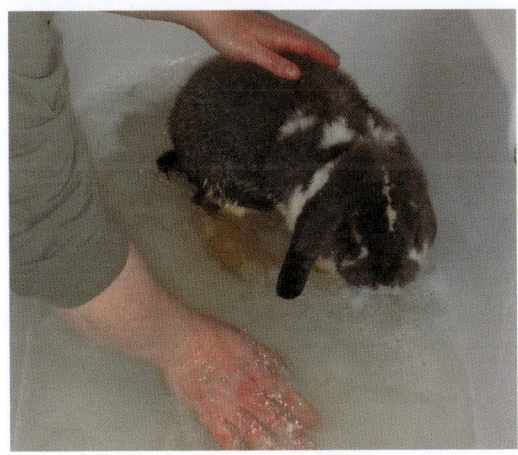

Urine scald – one of the few times when bathing a rabbit may be necessary

Vaccinations

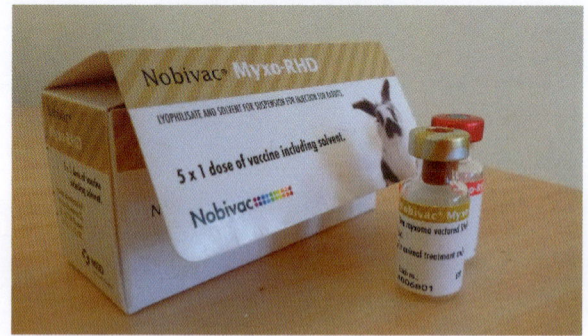

Combined Myxomatosis/VHD1 vaccine
(replaced in 2020 by Myxo-RHD Plus triple vaccine)

You are strongly urged to vaccinate your rabbit against both myxomatosis and VHD, viral haemorrhagic disease, also known as RHD, i.e. rabbit haemorrhagic disease.

A combined Myxo-RHD Plus vaccine was launched in the UK in spring 2020 replacing the earlier combined Myxo-RHD. This new vaccine provides the best protection against myxomatosis, VHD1 and the newer strain of VHD, i.e. VHD2.

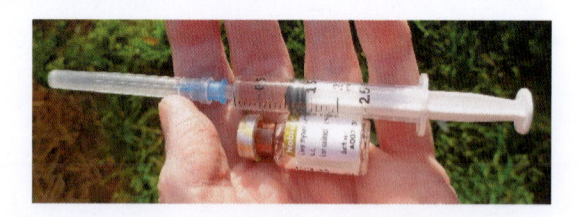

Myxomatosis

Myxomatosis is a type of pox virus which grows in the skin of rabbits.

The first indications of myxomatosis include:
- puffy, fluid swellings around the head and face
- 'sleepy' eyes
- swollen lips
- Hot, swollen ears with tenderness

- Puffy swellings around the genital area and anus

Within 1-2 days these swellings can increase and cause blindness.

The disease is spread by the rabbit flea which is frequently found on wild rabbits and can be transmitted by cats which come into contact with infected wild rabbits. However, is less easily spread by simple contact from one rabbit to another. If an infected rabbit shares a hutch with a healthy rabbit and neither have fleas then the disease is virtually never transmitted by simple contact.

Rabbit suffering puffy eyes and swollen ears of advanced myxomatosis

Myxomatosis – swollen genitals

The myxomatosis virus can remain dormant in the blood of fleas for several months. If a flea or flying insect should bite a rabbit then the virus is injected into the skin as the parasite sucks blood.

The virus is then transmitted to a local lymph node and enters the bloodstream enabling it to move around and multiply in the skin around the eyes, nose, face, ears and genitals. As the resulting swellings develop they make eating and drinking difficult and the swelling around the eyes causes blindness contributing to a prolonged death in some cases. Swellings around the nose can cause breathing difficulties and much discomfort.

The incubation period is 5-14 days. Some infected rabbits may survive for weeks while a more severely infected rabbit could succumb within 12 days. Very few wild rabbits will survive although pet rabbits, with dedicated owners, can very occasionally recover if they are intensively nursed, fed and watered and given antibiotics to prevent pneumonia. Recovery can take weeks or months and scarring, scaling and scabbing can persist on the head and body.

However, prevention is always better than cure and the spread of myxomatosis can be prevented or the risks minimised by:
- ensuring wild animals, and animals which might come into contact with wild animals/rabbits, do not come into contact with pet rabbits
- controlling fleas by use of sprays, dips, UV fly zappers and insect repellent strips
- ensuring bedding is always kept dry to avoid attracting mosquitoes
- Vaccination using the Nobivac Myxo-RHD Plus vaccine. Vaccination can give very good immunity but no vaccination can offer a complete guarantee of protection. Some rabbits may be immunologically incompetent and fail to respond the vaccination.

Rabbit with advanced myxomatosis. Photos by courtesy of K Brown

Rabbit Viral Haemorrhagic Disease (VHD-1, VHD-2)

Viral Haemorrhagic Disease is a very serious, fatal, disease which was first reported in the UK in 1992, has since spread throughout Britain and now mutated into a newer form, i.e. VHD2 (also known as RVHD2 and RHD2). It is very easily transmitted between rabbits or via contaminated food, bedding, hutches, birds, cats or even transmitted via owners e.g. on shoes or clothing. The virus can also survive outside a host for 3-4 months.

Generally, VHD affects rabbits aged over 6 weeks and symptoms include:

- loss of appetite
- nose bleeding
- breathing difficulties

The disease progresses rapidly and death usually occurs within 2 days, often without warning. In its acute form, it can be most distressing as blood clots develop on the lungs rendering the rabbit unable to breathe. Following death, there can be a frothy, bloodstained nasal discharge.

Some infected rabbits might squeal in pain. Like myxomatosis, there is no cure but the best possible protection is available via vaccination against both strains using the Myxo-RHD Plus vaccine.

When it's time to say Goodbye...

No matter how hard you try to save a severely ill, injured or aged much-loved rabbit, or indeed any pet, there comes a time when they are not going to recover and it is time to let them go.

This is one of the hardest tasks any pet owner has to face but you also have to ask - are you keeping the rabbit alive for their benefit, or for yourself and, given a choice, what would the rabbit choose? Or what would you choose if you were the rabbit?

Euthanasia

Animals are lucky. When they are terminally ill there is the option to end all suffering painlessly via euthanasia which leads to a peaceful, stress-free (for the rabbit) death rather than prolonged suffering or struggling.

Euthanasia involves the vet giving an overdose of anaesthetic so the rabbit becomes drowsy, falls asleep and slips away peacefully. Normally this is injected into a vein, often following a sedative which is administered first if the rabbit is stressed or in pain. The breathing slows, the rabbit relaxes, the eyes close and then s/he is gone. It is undoubtedly upsetting for an owner to watch but there can also be a sad feeling of relief too.

An alternative method used in the most severe cases involves in injection directly into the heart, following which the death is instant but this can be harder for an owner to watch.

When the time comes, most surgeries deal very compassionately with euthanasia and will arrange an appointment before or immediately following surgery hours so the owner doesn't have to sit in a busy waiting room knowing what's to follow. Some vets will give the injection in the owner's presence or take the rabbit to a back room. Before making the appointment, it is worth thinking through in advance whether or not you wish to be present.

If visiting a surgery is too stressful then many vets will make a home visit and euthanase in the rabbit's own home environment which can make the final appointment easier for you and your rabbit.

Cremation

Following euthanasia, or a natural death, there is then the option of cremation, either a single cremation whereby your rabbit's ashes will be returned to you in their own casket, or a shared cremation with other animals. The other alternative is to bury your rabbit in your garden complying with any local Council regulations regarding the depth of the grave.

It is never an easy time and it is natural to go through a grieving process. If your lost rabbit left behind a closely-bonded partner or companion then it is possible that the bereaved rabbit may pine so must be monitored closely for the next few days. It can also help both bereaved owners and partners to find a new rabbit to help fill the large gap the lost rabbit has left behind and to create new, happy memories as your move forwards.

I hope that you have found this
Grown-Up's Guide to
Caring for your Companion Rabbit
of help in caring for your rabbits

Copyright © 2021 Karen Wren
All Rights Reserved.

http://www.rossrabbits.co.uk
Email: rossrabbits@outlook.com

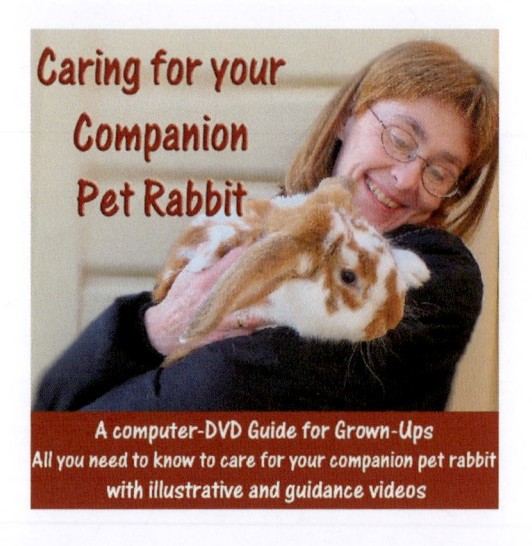

This Guide is also available on computer DVD:
**Caring for your Companion Pet Rabbit
- a DVD Guide for Grown-Ups**
with illustrative and guidance videos demonstrating how to handle your rabbit, check incisors, groom, clip claws, syringe-feed, give an injection and care for your rabbit's every need.

Order from: http://www.rossrabbits.co.uk/caredvd.html

Printed in Great Britain
by Amazon